STUDIES IN CLASSICAL LITERATURE, 9

THE EPODES
OF
HORACE

A STUDY IN POETIC ARRANGEMENT

by

ROBERT W. CARRUBBA

Columbia University

1969
MOUTON
THE HAGUE · PARIS

LIBRARY OF CONGRESS CATALOG CARD NUMBER 68-31897

Printed in The Netherlands by Mouton & Co., Printers, The Hague

Joanne
Vxori Optimae

χρῆμα θαυμαστὸν γυναικός

PREFACE

This little book of interpretative criticism attempts in its own way to pay *hommage* to one of Horace's most vital little books of poetry. The *Epodes* have in our own century and long before that not received the attention so exciting and varied a collection of poems deserves. There is no critical book in English devoted primarily to the *Epodes*. In German and French the last and only books went to press in 1904 and 1917 — too many years ago. Meanwhile, scholars have been at work in less ambitious publications. This present study, by incorporating not all but a considerable amount of the accumulated and worthwhile contributions to the appreciation of the *Epodes*, hopes to demonstrate that there is a great deal more of art and pleasure in the six hundred and twenty-five lines of seventeen epodes than has been suspected and that as much is easily discernible for those with eyes, time and concern. The nearly two hundred bibliographic citations may also prove useful to students, scholars and readers of Horace.

So many individuals and institutions are responsible in one way or another for this publication that to attempt simply to list all of them is beyond question. My gratitude is due to Professor James H. Reid of Fordham University under whom I first read Horace. My very sincere thanks are also extended to Professors George E. Duckworth and F. R. B. Godolphin of Princeton University who supervised, encouraged and criticized my dissertation from which this present study stems. Generous grants from the Danforth Foundation and Lake Forest College made possible its completion. Finally, to my parents and to my wife I am especially indebted for their kind understanding of my preoccupation with Horace.

New York City August 1965   R.W.C.

CONTENTS

REA	Revue des Études Anciennes
REG	Revue des Études Grecques
RFIC	Revista di Filologia e di Istruzione Classica
RhM	Rheinisches Museum für Philologie
RPh	Revue de Philologie
SIFC	Studi Italiani di Filologia Classica
SO	Symbolae Osloenses, auspiciis Societatis Graeco-Latinae
TAPA	Transactions of the American Philological Association
YClS	Yale Classical Studies
ZA	Zeitschrift für die Altertumswissenschaft
ZG	Zeitschrift für das Gymnasialwesen
ZRGG	Zeitschrift für Religions- und Geistesgeschichte

I

PRINCIPLES OF ARRANGEMENT

In attempting to uncover the principles governing the arrangement of the *Epodes* by Horace,[1] we are faced with no less than five possibilities:

1. Influence of the *Epodes* of Archilochus
2. Avoidance of any internal principle
3. Chronology
4. Metre
5. Theme

The first possibility I have already treated elsewhere,[2] and will again discuss the Archilochian question more fully after probing the remaining avenues of approach. The second possibility can with safety be dismissed in view of the research of Wilhelm Port[3] and others. That there existed among the Augustan poets an al-

---

[1] Horace himself surely arranged the *Epodes* as we now have them. Orelli-Baiter-Hirschfelder, *Q. Horatius Flaccus* 1 (Berlin, 1886), 614, comment: "Maxima pars horum epodorum referri debet ad genus illud, de quo ipse dixit epistl. I 19, 23: *Parios ego primus iambos Ostendi Latio numeros animosque secutus Archilochi, non res et agentia verba Lycamben.* Ex verbis ... patet has eclogas satis mature ab ipso poeta editas, non demum post eius mortem a grammatico aliquo collectas esse". That Horace intended very early to publish a book of epodes is clear from epode 14.6-8:
> Deus, deus nam me vetat
> Inceptos, olim promissum carmen, iambos
> Ad umbilicum adducere.

[2] See my "The Metrical Order of the Archilochian *Epodes*", *Emerita* 33 (1965), 61-70.

[3] "Die Anordnung in Gedichtbüchern augusteischer Zeit", *Philologus* 81 (1925), 280-308.

most fixed law that poems be artistically arranged in books is today beyond doubt, even if the principles of particular arrangements are frequently still matters of investigation and dispute.

II

CHRONOLOGY

The third possibility, chronology, may now occupy our attention and, as will quickly become clear, it too admits rapid discard. While Richard Bentley[1] did not argue in favor of a strict chronological arrangement of the *Epodes*, that is, that each succeeding epode is posterior in time to its numerical predecessor, he did claim that Horace composed his books in chronological order. Bentley's strict chronological scheme of Horace's works is:

WORK	POET'S AGE
Satires I	26-28
II	31-33
Epodes	34-35
Odes I	36-38
II	40-41
III	42-43
Epistles I	46-47
Odes IV and *Carmen Saec.*	49-51
Ars Poetica and *Epistles* II	uncertain

Thus, for Bentley, the *Epodes* were composed 31-30 B.C. Such a short period of composition, two years, might allow the inference that the seventeen epodes are themselves chronologically arranged. However, no less than four nineteenth century scholars[2] devoted sizeable studies to Horatian chronology, each in turn rejecting both

---

[1] *Q. Horatius Flaccus* (Cantabrigiae, 1711).

[2] C. Franke, *Fasti Horatiani* (Berlin, 1839), G. Grotefend, *Die schriftstellerische Laufbahn des Horatius* (Hannover, 1849). C. Kirchner, *Quaestiones Horatianae* (Numburgi, 1834). W. Teuffel, "Ueber die Abfassungszeit der Horazischen Epoden", *ZA* 64-66 (1844), 508-525; 75-77 (1845), 596-616.

the possibility of a two year period of composition and the possibility of a chronological arrangement of the *Epodes*. In our century, the major chronological study remains that of Rudolph Latsch.[3] Latsch has compiled two tables[4] which are significant for

Chronology of the *Epodes*

Epode	Kirchner	Franke	Grotefend	Teuffel	Latsch
1	31	31	31	31	32 (end)
2	30	30	35	30	30
3	33	35/34	34	36/35	36
4	38	38	38	38	36
5	34	37/36	40/39	38/37	38/37
6	35	—	38	40	41/40
7	31	32	32	41	38
8	39	40	39	41	40
9	31	31	31	31	31
10	34	—	38	40/38	38/37
11	37	34/33	34	37/38	35/34
12	40	36/35	39	40	40/39
13	32	—	31	43/40	36/34
14	33	33/32	34	34/33	32
15	33	33	38	41	41/38
16	41	41	32	41	36/35
17	32	30/29	39	37/36	36/35

Chronological Sequence of the *Epodes*

Kirchner	16	12	8	4	11	6	10	5	3	15	4	17	13	1	7	2
Franke	16	8	4	5	12	13	11	14	7	1	9	2	17			
Grotefend	5	17	12	8	10	6	4	15	2	3	14	11	7	16	1	13
Teuffel	7	16	13	15	8	6	12	10	4	5	17	11	3	14	1	2
Latsch	16	6	8	12	15	7	5	10	3	4	17	13	11	14	1	2

---

[3] *Die Chronologie der Satiren und Epoden des Horaz auf entwicklungsgeschichtlicher Grundlage* (Würzburg, 1936).
[4] *Ibid.*, 116-117.

the *Epodes*. Both summarize the findings of the four major nineteenth century studies as well as his own:

A glance at these two tables reveals that the consensus of critics (1) allows about a ten-year period for the composition of the *Epodes*, (2) rejects an overall chronological sequence of the *Epodes* (e.g., Kirchner, Franke and Latsch date epode 16 as the earliest poem), and (3) also rejects any partial chronological sequence (excepting Teuffel and Latsch's sequence of epodes 1 and 2 as the last composed).

III

METRE

Arrangement by the same or similar metre is unquestionably the most obvious and the most cogent principle operative in the *Epodes*. Franke, in dismissing chronology as a principle of arrangement, noted quite correctly: "In ordinandis epodis Horatium probabile est metrorum rationem habuisse. Certe hanc ob causam decem priores juxta se positi esse videntur."[1] But Franke, as well as other scholars, was led to the assertion of what appeared to be the logical corollary: "Nec in his neque in reliquis aut argumentum aut aetatem respexit." Hence, Franke's argument is simply that, where metre acts as the primary principle of arrangement, both chronology and theme may be discounted as ancillary principles. Franke, following Kirchner, did in fact disprove chronology as a factor; he did not, however, examine with care the possibility of a thematic principle superimposed upon a metrical one. Here our concern is with metre, but a caution that metrical arrangement need not exclude a thematic arrangement is necessary lest the reader be misled before the thematic question is discussed later in its proper place.[2]

---

[1] *Op. cit.* (above, n.II.2), 123.
[2] For the classic example in Horace see Walther Ludwig, "Zu Horaz, C. 2,1-12", *Hermes* 85 (1957), 336-345. Ludwig, building on the work of Port (above, n.I.3) uncovered a conscious cycle of twelve poems, at the beginning of book two of the *Odes*, in a structural chiasmus. Despite the fact that the first eleven poems are alternating alcaics and sapphics, the poet has not allowed this hard and fast metrical arrangement to completely dominate the arrangement of the poems. Hand in hand with the simple pattern of alternating metrics, Horace has contrived a more sophisticated and complex structure which at once cooperates with the arrangement by metre and superimposes

Let us first of all take notice of exactly which metres are employed and their order of employment in the *Epodes*:

Epode	Metre
1-10	A couplet consisting of iambic trimeter and iambic dimeter.

$$\breve{\times}: -\cup \mid -\breve{\times} \mid -\cup \mid -\breve{\times} \mid -\cup \mid -\wedge$$
$$\breve{\times}: -\cup \mid -\breve{\times} \mid -\cup \mid -\wedge$$

| 11 | Third Archilochian: a couplet consisting of iambic trimeter and elegiambus. |

$$\breve{\times}: -\cup \mid -\breve{\times} \mid -\cup \mid -\breve{\times} \mid -\cup \mid -\wedge$$
$$-\cup\cup \mid -\cup\cup \mid -\wedge \parallel \breve{\times}: -\cup \mid -\breve{\times} \mid -\cup \mid -\wedge$$

| 12 | Alcmanian Strophe: a couplet consisting of dactylic hexameter and dactylic tetrameter. |

$$-\cup\cup \mid -\cup\cup \mid - \parallel \cup\cup \mid -\cup\cup \mid -\cup\cup \mid -\circ$$
$$-\cup\cup \mid -\cup\cup \mid -\cup\cup \mid -\circ$$

| 13 | Second Archilochian: a couplet consisting of dactylic hexameter and iambelegus. |

$$-\cup\cup \mid -\cup\cup \mid - \parallel \cup\cup \mid -\cup\cup \mid -\cup\cup \mid -\circ$$
$$\breve{\times}: -\cup \mid -\breve{\times} \mid -\cup \mid -\wedge \parallel -\cup\cup \mid -\cup\cup \mid \underset{\smile}{\times}\wedge$$

| 14-15 | First Pythiambic: a couplet consisting of dactylic hexameter and iambic dimeter. |

$$-\cup\cup \mid -\cup\cup \mid - \parallel \cup\cup \mid -\cup\cup \mid -\cup\cup \mid -\circ$$
$$\breve{\times}: -\cup \mid -\breve{\times} \mid -\cup \mid -\wedge$$

| 16 | Second Pythiambic: a couplet consisting of dactylic hexameter and iambic trimeter. |

$$-\cup\cup \mid -\cup\cup \mid - \parallel \cup\cup \mid -\cup\cup \mid -\cup\cup \mid -\circ$$
$$\breve{\times}: -\cup \mid -\breve{\times} \mid -\cup \mid -\breve{\times} \mid -\cup \mid -\wedge$$

| 17 | Iambic Trimeter. |

$$\breve{\times}: -\cup \mid -\breve{\times} \mid -\cup \mid -\breve{\times} \mid -\cup \mid -\wedge$$

The basic metrical arrangement is readily apparent: 1-10 are couplets of iambic trimeter and dimeter; 11-16 are couplets of varied iambs and dactyls; 17 is iambic trimeter. Christ[3] suggested

---

upon it a thematic structural chiasmus. See also his "Die Anordnung des vierten Horazischen Odenbuches", *MH* 18 (1961), 1-10.

[3] W. Christ, *Horatiana* (Munich, 1893), 132, and note 1.

that Horace chose to begin his book with a round number of ten
poems of a simple Archilochian epodic metre and that the choice
of the number ten shows the influence of the *Idylls* of Theocritus
and the *Eclogues* of Vergil. The precise value of his suggestion
is questionable, especially in the case of Theocritus.[4] However,
what is certain is that epodes 1-10 comprise a purely iambic
group of the same metre. Looking at the table of metres, one
notes that the iambic character of the first metrical group of
epodes (1-10) is taken up again at the very beginning of the second
metrical group of varied iambs and dactyls (11-16) where in epode
11 the Third Archilochian begins with an iambic trimeter. This
first line is in fact the first line of the poems of the first metrical
group (1-10). The second line of epode 11 introduces for the first
time the dactylic note in the elegiambus. Thus epode 11 is transi-
tional, at once metrically linking the first and the second metrical
groups, for aside from epode 11, the second group, as Belling[5]
has noticed, shows a progression from dactyls to iambs:

Epode	Dactyls	Iambs
12	6+4	0
13	6+3	2
14-15	6	2
16	6	3

Epode 17 constitutes the third metrical group, a simple non-epodic
trimeter. Its relationship to the first two metrical groups is threefold: (1) it takes us back to the first line of the couplet of epodes
1-10; (2) it takes us back to the first line of the Third Archilochian,
the metre of epode 11 which begins the second metrical group
(11-16); and (3) it continues the progression from dactyls to iambs
in epodes 12-16, where epode 12 begins the series with 6+4

---

[4]   See, however, O. Skutsch, "The Structure of the Propertian *Monobiblos*",
CP 58 (1963), 238-239: "Augustan poets consider ten and multiples of five and
ten the ideal numbers for the poems of a book: the Cynthia Book-proper,
which consists of ... two double panels, conforms."
[5]   H. Belling, *Studien über die Liederbücher des Horatius* (Berlin, 1903), 137.

dactyls and 0 iambs and epode 16 ends the series with 6 dactyls and 3 iambs. Thus the book of epodes which began with pure iambics ends with pure iambics.[6]

[6] C. Giarratano, *Il libro degli Epodi* (Torino, 1930) viii, offers a somewhat different metrical division: "I primi undici epodi hanno come primo verso il trimetro giambico: nei primi dieci il secondo verso è il dimetro giambico, nell'undecimo l'elegiambo. Seguono cinque epodi che hanno come primo verso l'esametro, e i due epodi che hanno come secondo verso il dimetro giambico sono stati posti l'un dopo l'altro. L'ultimo componimento non è propriamente un epodo, ma è costituito da trimetri giambici κατὰ στίχον." Teuffel, *op. cit.* (above, n.II.2) 616, postulates a dual metrical division: 1-10 and 11-17. Both E. C. Wickham, *The Works of Horace*[3] 1 (Oxford, 1896), 26, and A. Kiessling and R. Heinze, *Oden und Epoden*[10] (Berlin, 1960), 486, accept the tripartite division presented above.

IV

THEME

Now that the basic principle of metrical arrangement has been accepted, the question of whether or not a thematic principle is likewise operative can properly be raised. Kirchner,[1] in the course of his careful refutation of Bentley's theory of chronological composition stated flatly: "Horatius in ordinandis singulis opusculorum suorum voluminibus certam legem vel a temporibus vel a rebus vel a personis petitam minime sibi impossuisse atque secutus esse videtur." Five years later, Franke[2] said essentially the same thing with particular reference to the *Epodes*. However, just one year prior to the publication of Franke's work, Cahn[3] had already noted that Horace in his various works had a tendency to place poems addressed to Maecenas in especially conspicuous places: the beginning, the middle and the end. Of the *Epodes* he said (his metrical division is dual):

Inter septemdecim epodos in ipso medio, qui est nonus, poeta principem illum amicorum suorum alloquitur, quumque septem, qui proprie epodi nominari non possint, seorsum in posteriore libri parte collocati sint, etiam horum ipsum medium, XIVmum dico, ad Maecenatem scriptum videmus.[4]

Taking his cue from Cahn, Teuffel further observed, at the very

---

[1] *Op. cit.* (above, n.II.2), 40.
[2] Above, 15-17.
[3] S. Cahn, *Trias Quaestionum Horatianarum* (Bonnae, 1838), 4-5. He cited: beginning, *Odes* 1.1, *Epodes* 1, *Sat.* 1.1, *Epist.* 1.1; middle, *Odes* 1.19 and 20 (the approximate center of 38 odes), 2.12 (close to the center of 20 odes) and 3.15 and 16 (of 30 odes), *Sat.* 1.5 and 6 (of 10 satires); end, *Odes* 2.20. 3.29, *Epist.* 1.19.
[4] *Ibid.*, 4-5.

beginning of his chronological study, that within the metrical division there was another principle operative: "Im Uebrigen scheint bei den zehn ersten Stücken auf eine solche Anordnung Bedacht genommen worden zu sein, bei welcher die dem Inhalt nach verwandten Gedichte von einander getrennt wurden."[5] Of this suggestion, more later.

Meanwhile, we have to deal with Belling's two attempts to discover the arrangement of the Epodes. Belling presented his first scheme in 1897 and his second in 1903. In the first,[6] Belling attempts to dislodge epodes 1 and 17 from the rest of the corpus and thus to leave a group of fifteen poems (2-16) capable of further division. Epode 1, he argues, (als wärmster Ausdruck des Verhaltnisses zu Maecenas) stands apart as a temperate poem and a dedicatory one, and 17 is likewise set apart because its metrics are not epodic. The remaining fifteen poems fall into two groups: a decade of two pentads, and an independent pentad. No comment or refutation of this attempted division is necessary since the author himself remarks in a subsequent publication:[7] "Mein Versuch, nach Absonderung von epo. I als Widmung und epo. 17 als Anhang, die übrigen als eine Dekade und eine Pentade aufzufassen, war verfehlt."

Belling's basic dissatisfaction with his first thematic division of the *Epodes* stems from his conviction that the threefold metrical division must furnish the guide lines for the thematic division. Hence, in his second division,[8] Belling found a coincidence of metrical and thematic divisions into three groups. The arrangements of groups A, B and C are:

A. 1-5, 6-10; B. 11-13, 14-16; C. 17.

Group A: The first decade is divided into two pentads. The first pentad: 1 a dedication to Maecenas; 2 a Vergilian glorification of the country man; 3 picks up the praise of simple country fare in 2.55-58 and exploits it, presenting Maecenas as the host. Thus 1-3

[5] *Op. cit.* (above, n.II.2), 616.
[6] H. Belling, *Untersuchung der Elegien des Albius Tibullus* (Berlin, 1897), 323-326.
[7] *Op. cit.* (above, n.III.5), 136.
[8] *Ibid.*, 136-141.

are a group placed deliberately at the head of the whole collection.
4 and 5 are two typical iambic pieces: 4 against a man and 5 against
a woman. Thus the overall structure of the first pentad is (1+2)
+ 2. The second pentad of group A: epode 6 differs in kind somewhat from epodes 4 and 5, for in this epode Horace attacks a
personal enemy after the fashion of Archilochus and Hipponax.
Similarly, the last epode (10) of the second pentad is directed
against a literary adversary, while 8 is again personal invective.
Thus the scheme of invective is 6, 8 and 10. Interspersed among
these three epodes are 7 and 9, two political poems, which correspond to one another: *Quo quo scelesti* and *Quando repostum
Caecubum.*

    Group B: This group of epodes divides itself into two parallel
triads. 11 and 14 correspond (11.1-2; 14.1-2, 5-8):

> Petti, nihil me sicut antea iuvat
>   scribere versiculos amore percussum gravi

and:

> Mollis inertia cur tantam diffuderit imis
>   oblivionem sensibus,
>
> . . . .
> candide Maecenas, occidis saepe rogando:
>   deus, deus nam me vetat
> inceptos, olim promissum carmen, iambos
>   ad umbilicum adducere.

A further correspondence is noted by Belling in *amor Lycisci me
tenet* (11.24) and *me ... Phryne macerat* (14.16). Epodes 12 and 15
also correspond: in 12 an old hag vainly courts the poet and in 15
Neaera is untrue to him. Finally 13 and 16 correspond as political
poems. Poem 17 (=Group C) would be a mere appendix were it
not connected in theme (Canidia) with epode 5.

    It must be said of Belling's division that it is neat; the basic
metrical and thematic groups correspond. Likewise, whereas
Group A is composed of ten poems which are divided into two
halves of five poems each, Group B is composed of six poems
which are divided into two halves of three poems each. A further
note of tidiness is found in the correspondence of the first three
poems of Group B with the second three poems of the same group

(11-13 and 14-16). This correspondence of halves of a group was absent in Group A. Epode 17, though a metrical oddity, may be connected with Group A through the Canidia theme.

Despite its neat symmetry and completeness, or more probably because of these, Belling's second arrangement will not hold good. Whereas in Belling's first attempt he found the decade 2-11 divided into two pentads (2-6 and 7-11), in his second attempt he found the decade 1-10 divided into two pentads (1-5 and 6-10). This is not to suggest that because his first division of a decade into two pentads failed that necessarily any later division of a different decade into pentads must likewise fail, but the sameness of approach does suggest that Belling was predisposed to find a pentadic division on his second attempt. The task at hand is to see if his second pentadic division is borne out by the poems themselves.

That poems 1-3 form, in a sense, a related group can be accepted at once; the discussion of what precisely this relationship is will be postponed to a more opportune time. Again one is inclined to admit the general relationship of 4 and 5 as "typical iambic invectives". But why epode 6 marks so sharp a division as to warrant beginning a second pentad with it remains unclear. Just as 4 is "against a man", so too is 6. Moreover, 4 and 6 are both poems of twenty lines of invective expressed in direct address. It has been observed that 4, 5 and 6 may form a group of invectives of which 4 and 6 of equal length and spirit bracket 5, the longest poem of the collection and an indirect attack in dramatic form.[9] Beyond this, the employment of the Archilochian animal motif in the very first lines of both 4 and 6 leads the reader to connect rather than to disassociate the two poems. Compare 4.1-2 with 6.1-2:

> Lupis et agnis quanta sortito obtigit
> tecum mihi discordia est

with:

> Quid immerentes hospites vexas canis
> ignavus adversum lupos?

Structurally, both 4 and 6 begin with a question and end with one. But the most cogent argument against the arrangement in two pentads is simply that it does not allow for the most obvious and

[9] W. Port, *op. cit.* (above, n.I.3), 292.

unquestionable relationship of epodes 1 and 9, the two Actium poems.

The arrangement of Group B (11-16) into two corresponding triads is no more successful. Epodes 11 and 14 undoubtedly admit a relationship which Belling pointed out: love prevents the poet from writing poetry. The relationship, however, of 12 and 15 is farfetched. 15's tone is heavily elegiac; that of 12 is fierce and bitter invective. The mate of 12 has always been and remains 8; their level is earthy and physical.[10] Of 15 Fraenkel[11] aptly remarked: "The principal theme of Epode XV is familiar from Elegy, and its dominating note of jealousy would not surprise us in Propertius."

Belling's pairing of 13 and 16 as political poems give rise to two objections. First, there is simply no evidence that 13 is in fact a political or war poem. In the case of the four known political epodes, 1, 7, 9 and 16, Horace makes it quite clear that he is dealing with national politics. The battle of Actium is the occasion for 1 and 9; 7 and 16 deal with civil war expressly. The case of 13 is quite different. We have a drinking song whose setting is a storm and whose philosophy is a genial epicurean exhortation to make the best of it while youth lasts and wine is at hand. A kind of divine providence (*deus*) may alter conditions for the better, but meanwhile *cetera mitte loqui* or, as Horace elsewhere says, *permitte divis cetera* (*Odes* 1.1.9), and let us lighten our hearts with song (13.1-10, 17-18):

> Horrida tempestas caelum contraxit et imbres
> nivesque deducunt Iovem; nunc mare, nunc silvae
> Threicio Aquilone sonant: rapiamus, amici,
> occasionem de die, dumque virent genua
> et decet, obducta solvatur fronte senectus.
> tu vina Torquato move consule pressa meo:
> cetera mitte loqui: deus haec fortasse benigna
> reducet in sede vice. nunc et Achaemenio
> perfundi nardo iuvat et fide Cyllenea
> levare diris pectora sollicitudinibus.

[10] For a careful and unbiased appraisal of the elements of various genres present in 8, 12 and 15, and how those of 8 and 12 differ from those of 15, see B. Kirn, *Zur literarischen Stellung von Horazens Jambenbuch* (Tübingen, 1935), 24-28, 49-52.

[11] E. Fraenkel, *Horace* (Oxford, 1957), 67.

In the last eight lines of the poem, Horace by way of a paradigm recalls Chiron's prophecy of Achilles' death and his advice to the hero (Horace's source is unknown):

> illic omne malum vino cantuque levato,
> deformis aegrimoniae dulcibus alloquiis.

Beyond what may be inferred from the text, and that is very little if anything, there is no evidence available for fixing the epode's date or occasion. A glance at the chronological chart of the Epodes[12] shows that this epode has been variously dated, 32, 31, 43/40 and 36/34, never with any cogent arguments. Belling[13] dates 13 about the time of 9 because he finds a similarity of thought between 13.5-6, 10 and 9.37-38:

> curam metumque Caesaris rerum iuvat
> dulci Lyaeo solvere.

This ignores the fact that the idea of dissolving one's cares with wine is a literary commonplace of antiquity and indeed of any culture which employs wine. The language of the two poems shows no special affinity. Hence, we are left with a poem whose occasion, aside from the coming of a storm, and date the poet has not troubled to tell us of, probably because the poem requires neither.

A final objection remains to be made against the association of 13 and 16. Just as the reader naturally associates 1 and 9 as the Actium poems and 8 and 12 as frank physical invectives, so too 7 and 16 are naturally related in that both are addresses on the part of the poet to the Roman people and both deal with the national suicidal horrors of civil strife. Where poems of so small a collection show a natural affinity, it seems pointless to ignore obvious relationship and to suggest in its place the unproven.

The famous study of Port, in so far as it dealt with the *Epodes*, was more modest in its findings on thematic arrangement.[14] Port accepted metre as the dominating principle of arrangement and evolved thematic relationships which adhered to the metrical divisions. Port, however, despaired of any thematic arrangement

---

[12] Above, 16.
[13] *Op. cit.* (above, n.IV.6), 324.
[14] *Op. cit.* (above, n.I.3), 292-296.

after the first ten epodes: "Darüber hinaus aber lässt sich eine
bewusste Ordnung nach dem Inhalt nicht mehr feststellen." In
poems 11-17, Port concluded, the metre offered a convenient
means of variety since only 14 and 15 employ the same metre:
"Die sieben Gedichte in sechs verschiedenen Massen stellte er
dahinter in der Weise, dass er allein das Metrum zur Richtlinie
der Ordnung nahm."

Within the metrical unit 1-10, Port argued a fourfold division
in which each successive group contains one more poem than its
predecessor:

$$\text{I} \mid \underbrace{\text{II} \quad \text{III}} \mid \underbrace{\text{IV} \quad \text{V} \quad \text{VI}} \mid \underbrace{\text{VII} \quad \text{VIII} \quad \text{IX} \quad \text{X}}$$

I is a dedication to Maecenas. II and III are counterparts, poems
of country life. II is an attack, whereby Horace, by placing the
praise of country life in the mouth of the *fenerator* Alfius, parodies
"die Schwärmerei des Städters für das Bauernleben, das er nur als
Sommerfrischler kennen gelernt hat (Kiessling-Heinze)". III, on
the other hand, is purely humorous, "die Erinnerung an ein harm-
loses Missgeschick". IV, V and VI are a group of poems of personal
attack. V, the Canidia poem, is the longest of the group and as an
attack on a woman it stands between two attacks on men (IV and
VI). VII, VIII, IX and X constitute an arrangement of two political
poems (VII and IX) and two personal attack poems (VIII and X) in
interlocked order.

Port's arrangement improves upon the second arrangement of
Belling in at least one respect. Port recognizes that, once a decision
has been made to consider 1-10 as a metrical and thematic unit
exclusive of 11-17, then poems 4, 5 and 6 form a group whose
object is personal attack. But if poem 5 is to be somewhat dif-
ferentiated from 4 and 6 primarily because 5 attacks a woman
(Canidia), then why should it not be connected with poem 8, the
only other poem of 1-10 which attacks a woman? Again, if poems
7 and 9 are associated as two political poems, should not epode 1
be included under the same heading? And if 4 and 6 are poems of
personal attack against men, does not 10, against the poet Mevius,
belong with them instead of being associated with epode 8 which

attacks a woman? The results are as follows and unimpressive
structurally:

I	II	III	IV	V	VI	VII	VIII	IX	X
a	b	b	c	d	c	a	d	a	c

a = political
b = country life
c = attack against a man
d = attack against a woman

Walter Wili[15] was equally unimpressed with not only the idea of
a patterned arrangement of 1-10 but also of the entire book.
Wili's basic metrical arrangement is 1-10 and 11-17, with 1 serving
as a dedication to Maecenas of Group A (1-10) as well as the whole
book, and 11 serving as a subordinate dedication to Pettius of
Group B (11-17). He points out that 1, 3 and 14 are light and turn
about Maecenas or play on his friendship, just as 9, 11, 13 and 15
betray the poet's maturity and later art. Heavy scorn predominates
in 4, 5, 8, 10, 12 and 17, while it appears incidentally or in a playful
manner in 2, 6, 15, 3, 7 and 16. He comments:

Zugleich aber ist dem Anordnungsprinzip der variatio Genüge getan;
denn nur einmal stehen Gedichte ähnlichen Charakters und Spottes
nebeneinander, die Stücke 4 und 5; sonst reihen sich die in Geist und
zeitlicher Abfassung verschiedenen. Horaz folgt damit nur einem Stilprinzip seiner Epoche — denn die Gedicht-Anordnung ist für die römischen Dichter ein Stilprinzip — und er ist hierin zeitlebens Meister
geblieben.

Aside from the relationship of 6 to 4 and 5, already noted, other
objections may be made to Wili's remarks.[16] For Wili, a patterned
arrangement is absent because, he claims, the poems which follow
one another are different in character and time of composition.
But the matter of character involves questions of theme and tone,
which he has only partially explored. Again, time of composition
is only one criterion of association; nor can immediate juxtaposition of related poems be argued the single form of a pattern.
Two basic patterns of Horatian word order are in fact the chiasmus

[15] *Horaz und die augusteische Kultur* (Basel, 1948), 45-53.
[16] Epodes 2 and 3 are also related, but this relationship is more conveniently
discussed later.

and interlocked,[17] in which the words may or may not be juxtaposed.
It is now clear that no patterned arrangement which respects fundamental relationships of poems has been successfully argued for the *Epodes*.[18] Neither Belling's pentads and triads which nicely accounted for every epode nor Wili's principle of *variatio* which allowed for almost no relationships are satisfactory. There are ever present the pitfalls of seeing pattern everywhere and, failing a complete pattern, of seeing pattern nowhere.

Determining thematic or other relationships is at best a hazardous affair. The human mind seeks to order chaos and rests easy when a pattern is clear; the danger is that the order or pattern may be present in the mind but not in reality. This danger increases as the investigation becomes more exclusively personal. For this reason, caution demands that we present a representative listing of thematic groupings of the *Epodes*:

---

[17] See H. D. Naylor, *Horace. Odes and Epodes. A Study in Poetic Word-Order* (Cambridge, 1922), xiii, and G. Brunori, *La lingua d'Orazlo* (Firenze, 1930), 126-127.

[18] Mention should also be made of several other views of the arrangement of the *Epodes*. A Siess, *Zu den Epoden des Horaz* (Graz, 1875), 26, notes two main groups of epodes: 5, 6, 8, 10, 12, 17, 4, 7, 16 "... in denen Horaz seiner Erbitterung und seinem Unwillen Luft macht"; and 2, 3, 11, 13, 14, 15, 1, 9 "... in welchen er entweder heiteren Humor zum Ausdruck bringt, oder in denen Gedanke und Diction bereits den höheren Schwung der Lyrik zeigen." Further, he argues, 5, 6, 8, 10, 12, 17 are directed against particular persons from Horace's personal motives; 4, 7, 16 express political indignation. Of the second group, 11, 13, 14, 15, 1, 9 show a decided lyric stamp. W. Kroll, *Studien zum Verständnis der römischen Literatur* (Stuttgart, 1924), 228, comments: "In den Epoden stehen zehn Gedichte derselben Form, aber dann folgen sieben in verschiedenen Massen; die eigentlichen aggressiven iambi (4. 6. 8. 10. 12), die politischen Gedichte (7. 13. 16), die mimenartigen (2. 5. 17), die an Maecenas gerichteten (1. 3. 9. 14), die Liebeslieder (11. 15) sind symmetrisch über das Buch verteilt." M. Schmidt, "Das Epodenbuch des Horaz", *PhW* 52 (1932), 1005-1010, presents another arrangement of the *Epodes*, one which, it seems to me, ignores considerations of both theme and tone. She would have us take epodes 1-4 as containing two pairs of poems (1-2 and 3-4), the first of each pair being what she calls "personal" and the second of each pair being "general". Epodes 5 and 6 are again a pair according to the same (by a complicated application of the terms "subjective" and "objective") principle. 7 introduces a national theme and 8 continues the pattern of 2, 4 and 6. 9 and 10 are the last of the five pairs; the interest of 9 is personal and that of 10 (against Mevius!) is general. For epodes 11-17, she accepts Belling's second division.

Plüss:[19]

A. Personal Life: 1, 3, 13, 15
B. Literary Life: 10, 11, 14, 17
C. Social and Moral: 2, 4, 6, 8, 12
D. Political or National: 5, 7, 9, 16

Olivier:[20]

A. Against Women: 8 and 12 against two old women, le bas-bleu
   et l'amoureuse; 5 and 17 against Canidia
B. Against Personal Enemies: 4, 6, 10
C. Political: 7, 9, 16
D. To Maecenas: 1, 2, 3
E. Confessions of Love: 11, 15
F. Passage to Lyric Poetry: indicated by 14, effected by 13

Campbell:[21]

A. Lampoons: 4, 5, 6, 8, 10, 12, 17
B. Playful: 2, 3
C. Erotic: 11, 14, 15
D. Political: 1, 7, 9, 13, 16

Port:[22]

A. Political: 1, 7, 9, 16
B. Personal Attack: 5 and 17 against Canidia; 8 and 12 against
   an odious old woman; 4, 6, 10 against men
   (2 and 3, contrary pictures of country life)
C. Love and the Enjoyment of Life: 11, 13, 14, 15

Villeneuve:[23]

A. Personal Attack: 4, 5, 6, 8, 10, 12, 17
B. Plaisantes ou Railleuses: 2, 3
C. Civic: 7, 9, 16
D. Amoureuses et Bachiques: 11, 14, 15, 13

[19] T. Plüss, *Das Jambenbuch des Horaz* (Leipzig, 1904), 129-130.
[20] F. Olivier, *Les Épodes d'Horace* (Lausanne, 1917). Olivier, 52, contends
that A and B include only free invective, but that A, B, C are more open than
the following three groups (D, E, F) whose tone is more intimate.
[21] A. Y. Campbell, *Horace. A New Interpretation* (London, 1924), 128-135.
[22] *Op. cit.* (above, n.I.3), 293-294.
[23] F. Villeneuve, *Horace. Odes et Épodes* (Paris, 1927), 195-198.

E. Qui échappe à toute classification: 1

Giarratano:[24]

A. Political and Civic: 7, 9, 16
B. Maecenas: 1, 3
C. Invective: 2, 4, 5, 6, 8, 10, 12, 17
D. Love: 11, 14, 15
E. Anguish: 13

Kirn:[25]

A. Direkte Invektive: 4, 6, 8, 10, 12
B. Zaubergedichte (eingekleidete Invektive): 5, 17
C. Παίγνια mit bukolischen Einschlag: 2, 3
D. Politische Gedichte: 7, 9, 16
E. Persönliches Gedicht an Mäzenas (mit politischem Einschlag): 1
F. Liebesgedichte: 11, 14, 15
G. Trinklied: 13

Fraenkel:[26]

A. In the Iambist's Manner: 2, 10; 4, 6, 8, 12 (fierce invective);
                                    5, 17 (Canidia); 7, 16 (political)
B. Not in the Iambist's Manner: 3, 11, 13, 14, 15
C. The Two Actium Poems: 1, 9

The following chart with accompanying notes will make clear the areas of *communis opinio* (pp. 34-35).

A glance at the chart will show the unanimous agreement on the grouping of 7, 9 and 16 as national or political poems. The position of epode 1 poses a problem. Campbell, Port, Kirn and Fraenkel easily associate it with 9; Fraenkel refers to 1 and 9 as "The Two Actium Poems", Belling, Olivier and Giarratano consider it an epode to Maecenas, while Villeneuve claims that it

---

[24] *Op. cit.* (above, n.III.6) viii. Gairratano notes that Horace's person is always present, except in 2 and 5 where there is no direct reference to the poet. But when 5 is connected with 17, it acquires a personal involvement.
[25] *Op. cit.* (above, n.IV.10), 12
[26] *Op. cit.* (above, n.IV.11), 24-75.

escapes classification. But the most intimate relationship which exists between 1 and 9 is clear when the poems are read the one after the other.

On the most obvious level both poems are concerned with the same three people: Horace, Maecenas and Octavian, and their common occasion is the battle of Actium, 31 B.C. In epode 1, Horace expresses his desire to accompany Maecenas on the Liburnian gallies amid the lofty battlements of ships. Even as Maecenas shares the dangers of Caesar, so too would Horace for friendship's sake share those of Maecenas. In 9, Horace again addresses Maecenas. This time, however, he wonders when the two will drink to Caesar's victory over Antony and Cleopatra. The exact time and locale of epode 9 are much disputed, but for our purposes whether Horace was actually at Actium (on the hill or at sea) or remained at Rome is not important.[27] What is important is that 1 and 9 are companion pieces.

Let us compare the first four lines of both poems (1.1-4 and 9.1-4):

> Ibis Liburnis inter alta navium,
>   amice, propugnacula,
> paratus omne Caesaris periculum
>   subire, Maecenas, tuo.

and:

> Quando repostum Caecubum ad festas dapes
>   victore laetus Caesare
> tecum sub alta — sic Iovi gratum — domo,
>   beate Maecenas, bibam

The name Caesar occurs only four times in the *Epodes*, once in 1 and three times in 9. In epode 1, Maecenas is *paratus omne Caesaris*

---

[27] On this problem, see especially E. Wistrand, *Horace's Ninth Epode* (Göteborg, 1958). Wistrand, 19, writes: "The conclusion is: there is not reliable external evidence to help us determine where and when Horace wrote his ninth epode. We have nothing to go by but the poem itself." Elsewhere, 35, Wistrand comments: "The ninth epode is a counterpart to the first. In this the poet protests his eagerness to follow his friend Maecenas into the perils of war; in our epode he represents himself as sharing with Maecenas the anxieties of war," See also my "The Structure of Horace's Ninth Epode", *SO* 41 (1966), 98-107.

	Political or National	Invective	Erotic and Sympotic
Belling[28]	7 9 13 16	4 5 6 8 10 12 17	11 14 15
Pluss[29]	5 7 9 16	2 4 6 8 12	
Olivier[30]	7 9 16	4 5 6 8 10 12 17	11 13 14 15
Campbell[31]	1 7 9 13 16	4 5 6 8 10 12 17	11 14 15
Port[32]	1 7 9 16	(2) (3) 4 5 6 8 10 12 17	11 13 14 15
Villeneuve[33]	7 9 16	4 5 6 8 10 12 17	11 13 14 15
Giarratano[34]	7 9 16	2 4 5 6 8 10 12 17	11 14 15
Kirn[35]	1 7 9 16	4 5 6 8 10 12 17	11 13 14 15
Fraenkel[36]	1 7 9 16	4 5 6 8 10 12 17	11 13 14 15

[28] Belling presents no formal thematic grouping of the *Epodes* independent of his pentadic and triadic arrangement, but his remarks indicate this classification. See above, 23-27.

[29] Plüss, *op. cit.* (above, n.IV.19), 133-135, considers 5 a political allegory on the great occasion of the era, the union of old Rome with the foreign enchantress Cleopatra; 17, composed after the death of Antony and Cleopatra, is iambic poetry intensified in metre, content and tone to the severest parody of the tragic drama. Plüss does associate 2 and 3 as poems on country life composed about the same time. Following the approach of Plüss, R. C. Kukula, *Römische Säkularpoesie. Neue Studien zu Horaz'* 16. *Epodus und Vergils* 4. *Ekloge* (Leipzig, 1911), 40 note 5, concludes: "Die Erkenntnis des Archilochischen Characters des XVI. Epodus weist uns die Richtung für die Interpretation aller übrigen Epoden, in denen man bis heute nichts oder nur wenig 'Aggressives' finden will. Kein Zweifel, dass auch die Stücke I, II, IX, XIII, XIV verfeinertes iambisches Ethos zeigen, bald in harmloser Neckerei oder humorvoller Selbstverspottung, bald in lachender Ironie oder ernsthaftem Tadel." The critical weakness of the Plüss methodology was nicely pointed out by one of his reviewers, R. Cahen, *Bulletin Critique* 5 (1905), 91-97: "Mais on y voit clairement comment l'abus de l'érudition empêche l'examen personnel et impartial du texte, comment l'abus des abstractions (qui vient d'un désir facheux de mêler les idées et les sentiments modernes dans l'interpretation des œuvres antique) affaiblit les intuitions qui se dégagent d'une œuvre concrète minutieusement étudiée, comment enfin la subtilité, le besoin de tout savoir et de tout deviner, fait perdre la juste mesure."

[30] "Invective" includes Olivier's poems "Against Women" and "Against Personal Enemies". Similarly, "Erotic and Sympotic" includes his "Confessions of Love" and "Passage to Lyric Poetry".

[31] Like Belling, Campbell, *op. cit.* (above, n.IV.21), 143, considers 13 a

Country Life: Playful	To Maecenas	Personal Life	Literary Life	Anguish	Escapes Classification
2 3	1				
(2) (3)		1, 3, 13, 15	10, 11, 14, 17		
	1 2 3				
2 3					
2 3					
2 3					1
	1 3			13	
2 3					
2 3					

political poem: "That the inclement weather which provides the ostensible occasion for the thirteenth is a symbol for political storm and anxiety is indicated later in the poem itself (7-8) [cetera mitte loqui: deus haec fortasse benigna / reducet in sedem vice]. The political application, indeed, has been otherwise explained [while Horace was in Greece in the service of the republican forces under Brutus]; but as on this count we are practically required to date the piece very early if we do not put it among the latest, I prefer the latter alternative, on the ground that this is the only one of the epodes which in style and diction, as well as in its hortatory tone resembles the more serious type of Ode; so much that it could be placed among the Odes without any incongruity."

[32] Port, op. cit. (above, n.I.3), 294, notes at the end of his group, Personliche Angriffe: "Hier seinen die eng zusammengehörigen Gedichte II und III eingereiht, die gegensätzliche Bilder aus dem Landleben geben."

[33] Villeneuve, op. cit. (above, n.IV.23), 198, comments: "J'ai réservé l'épode 1, qui échappe à toute classification et se place à côté des odes où s'exprime le mieux l'amitié d'Horace pour Mécène."

[34] The classification of 13 is curious. After discussing the grouping of the other poems, Giarratano, op. cit. (above, n.III.6), viii, says of Horace: "o parla dei suoi amori (11, 14 e 15) o delle sua angosce (13)," A connection of 11, 14 and 15 with 13 was perhaps intended. See xii.

[35] "Invective" includes what Kirn, op. cit., (above, n.IV.10), 12, terms "Direkte Invektive" (4, 6, 8, 10, 12) and "Zaubergedichte" = "eingekleidete Invektive" (5, 17). "Political or National" includes 1 as a "Persönliches Gedicht an Mäzenas mit politischem Einschlag".

[36] For the linking of 1 and 7 with 9 and 16 see Fraenkel, op. cit. (above, n.IV. 11) 70-71; for the classification of 2 see 60-61. On the tone of epode 3, see 69.

periculum subire, where the name Caesar occurs at line three before
Horace has in fact named the addressee of the poem, Maecenas. In
9, *Caesare* is placed at the end of line two, again before the addressee of the poem, Maecenas, is named at line 4. Whereas in 1
Horace dwells more on his relationship with his patron, Caesar is
the focal point of 9. The *Caesare* of line 2 is picked up again at line
18 where the *Galli* are described as *canentes Caesarem* and again
at line 37 with:

> curam metumque Caesaris rerum iuvat
> dulci Lyaeo solvere.

Notice the careful symmetrical positioning of the name Caesar;
lines 2, 18 and 37: the second from the beginning, the central
position (line 18 of 38 lines), and the second line from the last.

In the case of the name Maecenas the parallel is even stronger.
The name occurs only once in each poem: in both cases this is
line 4:

> subire, Maecenas, tuo

and:

> beate Maecenas, bibam

The exact duplication of linear position is matched by that of
metrical position: syllables 4, 5 and 6 of an iambic dimeter line,
leaving three syllables before and two syllables after the vocative.
The use of a second term with Maecenas furnishes another parallel.
In 1.2 *amice* may be either a vocative noun further specified by the
proper name Maecenas or a vocative adjective employed in a
hyperbaton.[37] In 9.4 *beate* stands immediately before and adjectiv-
ally qualifies Maecenas. In *inter alta navium, amice, propugnacula*
and *sub alta — sic Iovi gratum — domo* there is another indication
that in composing 9.1-4 Horace had in mind 1.1-4. In the first
instance Maecenas will journey *inter alta … propugnacula*; in the
second Horace wishes to drink *sub alta … domo*. In both instances
the noun (*propugnacula* and *domo*) is separated from its preposition

---

[37]   E. Fraenkel, *op. cit.* (above, n.IV.11), 69 note 1, argues against a hyperbaton. Fraenkel comments on Horace's manner of introducing Maecenas:
"… he begins with an allusive characterization and, after an interval (some-
times a long one), lets the name follow."

followed by the modifying adjective by the unexpected intrusion of a jarring word or phrase: *amice* and *sic Iovi gratum*. Though one might expect the phrase *alta domus* in one case or another to occur as a commonplace in Horace, the phrase in fact occurs only once elsewhere in Horace, *Serm.* 2.6.114, composed about the same time as *Epodes* 1 and 9, where the locale is a wealthy mansion at Rome, the habitat of the town mouse.

Horace's question: *Quando repostum Caecubum ... bibam* was answered by himself in *Odes* 1.37: *Nunc est bibendum.* The poet did not forget his brand of wine (*ibid.*, 4-5): *antehac nefas depromere Caecubum cellis avitis.* Again in 1.37 the name Caesar has been carefully placed. It occurs once in the ode at its center, line sixteen of thirty-two lines, just as it occurred at the center of epode 9.[38] Epode 9 and ode 1.37 are so intimately and patently related that a demonstration of this relationship is here unnecessary. It is, however, worth noticing that 1.37 will also recall for us epode 1. In epode 1, Maecenas was to set forth in *Liburnis*; in the ode, Cleopatra is pictured as (30-32):

saevis Liburnis scilicet invidens
privata deduci superbo
non humilis mulier triumpho.

These are the only occurrences of the word *Liburnus* in the poetry of Horace.

Critics who classify epode 1 under the headings "To Maecenas", "Personal Life" or "Escapes Classification" are not really rejecting the poem's relation to epode 9, but rather they are pointing up the expressed intimacy and genuine friendship of Horace and Maecenas which are at the core of epode 1. In 9 there is a shift of emphasis. The intimacy and friendship are still present, but whereas in 1 Horace was prepared to go to Actium for Maecenas' sake even as Maecenas himself was prepared to go for Caesar's sake, in epode 9 the relationship of Horace and Maecenas is taken for granted and a victorious Caesar is at the core of the poem as the burst of praise at the poem's heart proclaims: *Galli, canentes Caesarem.* In

---

[38] Beyond doubt the placement of the addressees, *sodales*, of the ode at line 4 is calculated. It recalls by position chiefly Horace's especial *sodalis*, Maecenas, addressed at *Epodes* 1.4 and 9.4.

epode 1, we have Horace's direct and blunt protestation of friendship for Maecenas in the setting of Caesar's peril; in 9, Horace
shares unselfconsciously his anxiety over the *curam metumque
Caesaris rerum* with Maecenas. In this sense and on the basis of
the verbal similarities discussed, one can call epodes 1 and 9 companion pieces.

Along with 1 and 9, epodes 7 and 16 complete the group of
political or national poems. The critics to a man are in accord
in asserting the relationship of 7 and 16. Little therefore needs to
be said about the two poems. Like 1 and 9, 7 and 16 deal with
civil strife; in the first instance the principals are Horace, Maecenas
and Caesar, and the occasion is Actium, in the second the principals
are Horace and the Roman people, and the occasion is the renewal
of civil war, not further concretized.

Lines 1-10 of epodes 7 and 16 also display evidence of one being
composed with the other in mind, as was the case of lines 1-4
of epodes 1 and 9. Unfortunately, the chronology of 7 and 16
is far from fixed, so that it is impossible to decide which poem
influenced which. As indicated on Latsch's chart of the chronology
of the *Epodes*, 7 has been variously dated in the years 31, 32 (twice),
41 and 38, while 16 has been dated with more agreement in the
years 41 (three times), 32 and 41/40. Opinion, while varied, generally agrees that epode 16 preceded 7, and Kirchner, Franke and
Latsch consider it the earliest of all the epodes. For this reason,
though either chronology does not invalidate the similarities, let
us cite 16.1-10 first and then 7.1-10:

> Altera iam teritur bellis civilibus aetas,
>   suis et ipsa Roma viribus ruit;
> quam neque finitimi valuerunt perdere Marsi
>   minacis aut Etrusca Porsenae manus,
> aemula nec virtus Capuae nec Spartacus acer
>   novisque rebus infidelis Allobrox,
> nec fera caerulea domuit Germania pube
>   parentibusque abominatus Hannibal,
> impia perdimus devoti sanguinis aetas,
>   ferisque rursus occupabitur solum.
>
> Quo, quo scelesti ruitis? aut cur dexteris
>   aptantur enses conditi?

      parumne campis atque Neptuno super
        fusum est Latini sanguinis,
      non, ut superbas invidae Carthaginis
        Romanus arces ureret,
      intactus aut Britannus ut descenderet
        Sacra catenatus via,
      sed ut secundum vota Parthorum sua
        urbs haec periret dextera?

The first two lines of 16 tell us in a declarative statement that
another age is being destroyed by civil war and that *suis et ipsa Roma
viribus ruit*. In line 1 of 7 the verb is repeated in an impatient
question: *Quo, quo scelesti ruitis*, while the adjective-noun pairs
suis et ipsa Roma viribus find their parallels in 7.9-10: *sua urbs haec
dextera*. Epode 16 repeats the word *aetas* at the end of lines 1 and
9; epode 7 repeats the word *dexter* at the end of lines 1 and 10.[39]
The notes of guilt (*scelesti*) and blood (*Latini sanguinis*) in 7
reflect the same in 16.9, *impia aetas* and *devoti sanguinis*. 7.17-20
nicely contain the idea:

      sic est: acerba fata Romanos agunt
        scelusque fraternae necis,
      ut immerentis fluxit in terram Remi
        sacer nepotibus cruor.

Structurally, epode 16 devotes the first two lines to two declarative
statements followed by six lines comprising a roll call of formidable
Roman enemies (Marsi, Etrusci, Capua, Spartacus, Allobrox,
Germania and Hannibal) who were unable to effect the destruction
of Rome — a feat now being accomplished by the Romans themselves. Epode 7 devotes its first two lines to two interrogative
statements and allots six lines (5-10) to a roll call of three foes
(Carthago, Britannus and Parthia) against whom Roman swords
might better be directed. Let us content ourselves with noting one
final parallel of many that could be noted. 16 implies as its setting
some sort of fictitious gathering of Romans at which Horace is
addressing his countrymen. He poses a question: *sic placet? an
melius quis habet suadere?* (23) to which no answer is given and the
poet is left content with his own answer. The setting of epode 7

---

[39]   The exact forms are *dexteris* and *dextera*. The numbers of the substantives
are made to agree with the numbers of the subjects, *enses* and *Roma*.

is less clear, but the poet is again addressing his own countrymen. He poses a question: *furorne caecus, an rapit vis acrior, an culpa?* and demands an answer: *responsum date* (13-14). No answer is given (*tacent* at line 15), and Horace is left content with his own (*sic est* at 17).

Of the group of poems classified as invective, those attacking Canidia (5 and 17) are most easily associated. They are by far the longest epodes, 102 and 81 lines, respectively. The scene of 5 is laid at a Roman house where Canidia is about to sacrifice a young boy so that his cut and dried marrow and liver may furnish a love philtre to win over her reluctant lover Varus, a *senem adulterum*. The whole results in a horror-farce arranged in a chiasmus (according to the allocation of lines to Horace as the narrator and to the *puer*) which brackets Canidia's incantation, the poem's central focus:

Lines	Speaker
1-10	Puer———————
11-49	Horace————
49-82	Canidia
83-86	Horace————
87-102	Puer———————

The basic structure of 17 is simple, a mock palinode composed of a speech by Horace addressed to Canidia (1-52) begging that she end her magic[40] spells against him, and Canidia's scornful refusal (53-81). The whole is a tongue-in-cheek affair in which all the offensive charges that Horace says he wishes to take back are in fact naïvely confirmed by Canidia herself. The persistent note of humor provides relief after the horror and pathos of epode 5.

The relative chronology of the three Canidia poems cannot be fixed with absolute certainty. However, there is little doubt that the sequence is: epode 5, *Sat.* 1.8 and epode 17. The poems are related by more than their common theme. Epode 5, as noted, centers on Canidia's speech which is bracketed by two descriptions

---

[40]   For Canidia's magic see L. Fahz, *De poetarum romanorum doctrina magica* (Numburgi, 1904), and J. F. d'Alton, *Horace and His Age. A Study in Historical Background* (London, 1917), 198-221.

by Horace and two speeches by the *puer*. Satire 1.8 is a dramatic monologue by Priapus. Epode 17 is composed of two set speeches, one by Horace and the other by Canidia. Aside from the usual arguments adduced for the priority of epode 5 to satire 1.8, there is another indication within the poems helpful in establishing their sequence. The young boy's last prophecy to Canidia and her accomplices was (*Epodes* 5.97-102):

> vos turba vicatim hinc et hinc saxis petens
> contundet obscenas anus;
> post insepulta membra different lupi
> et Esquilinae alites;
> neque hoc parentes, heu mihi superstites
> effugerit spectaculum.

When we next meet Canidia in the works of Horace, she is indeed upon the Esquiline — not dead — but in the act of calling forth by incantations the shades of the dead buried in that pauper's and criminal's cemetery and shortly to be routed by the cracking of a wooden image of Priapus (*Sat.* 1.8.24-50).

Epode 17 is the last composed of the three. That it is subsequent to epode 5 is clear: the barb of 5.5-6 is ironically apologized for in 17.50-52:

> tuusque venter Pactumeius, et tuo
> cruore rubros obstetrix pannos lavit,
> utcumque fortis exsilis puerpera.

Similarly, Canidia's threat (17.56-57) that Horace's publicizing and mockery of the rites of Cotytia shall not go unavenged arises from Horace's exposé in epode 5. The next two lines of epode 17 (58-59) deal with the second poem offensive to Canidia, satire 1.8:

> et Esquilini pontifex venefici
> impune ut Vrbem nomine impleris meo?

The *cereas imagines* and *possim crematos excitare mortuos* of 17.76, 79 refer us again to the witchcraft at the Esquiline cemetery which Horace is charged with witnessing (*ut ipse nosti curiosus*).[41]

---

[41] Kirchner, *op. cit.* (above, n.II.2), 27, says of epode 17: "Hanc enim Eclogam et post Epod. 5. et post Sat. 8. scriptam esse, inde manifesto apparet, quod probra in utraque Canidiae objecta hic respiciuntur, nam v. 49. 56. 57. 80. ad illum Epodum, v. 47. 48. 59. 76-79. ad hanc Satiram spectant."

Canidia does elsewhere receive occasional insults in passing. In *Sat.* 2.1.48 she, among others, is taken as an illustration of the principle that by natural law each creature attacks employing the weapon with which it is strong:

> Canidia Albuci quibus est inimica venenum [minitatur]

In epode 3, Horace wonders if Canidia has tampered with the food which made him ill (3.7-8 where Canidia is juxtaposed with another witch, Medea, perhaps to prepare the audience for the full treatment of Canidia in epode 5). The last passing reference is most interesting, for it may contain an indication as to the relative chronology of the publication of the *Epodes* and *Satires* 2. Satire 8, the last satire of book two, treats the ostentatious and vulgar dinner given by the tasteless host, Nasidienus. The guest victims eventually take their revenge on their garrulous host by departing without tasting his dishes — and Horace adds a curious tag (94-95):

> ut nihil omnino gustaremus, velut illis
> Canidia adflasset peior sepentibus Afris.[42]

With these words ends the second book of satires. And we must ask ourselves why. Was it purely a parting shot, a last arbitrary flippant remark, aimed at one of many convenient wretches? Possibly, but I think not. Its function is twofold. First, by position in the eighth satire of book two it recalls the eighth satire of book one, Canidia on the Esquiline.[43] But within the material of the eighteen satires Canidia does not figure significantly enough to demand that the whole collection end with a reference to her. What I am suggesting is that Horace had an additional motive — he chose to let fly another barb at Canidia in his last line of his last satire so that it also might recall for us another of his works — the *Epodes* in which Canidia figures as the subject of the two longest

---

[42] Columella, *de re rustica* 8.5.18: cavendumque ne a serpentibus [pulli] adflentur, quarum odor tam pestilens est, ut interimat universos.

[43] A. Kurfess, "Vergil und Horaz", *ZRGG* 6 (1954), 359-364, contends, 363: "Horaz polemisiert in Epod. 5 und 17 und Sat. I 8 gegen die vergilische erotisch-sentimental stimmungsvolle Hexendarstellung (Buc. VIII), der er äusserst realistisch gesehene abstossende Vetteln entgegenstellt, die auch durchaus verbrecherisch sind." More probably *Sat.* 1.8 by its position and theme was meant merely to recall *Eclogues* 8.

poems, 5 and 17, whose total of 183 lines represents about 25%
of the 625 total number of lines in the *Epodes*. The connection of
food and Canidia, as already mentioned, occurs in epode 3. More
important, however, is position. It is entirely probable that either
the *Epodes* had already been published before the second book of
satires or that they existed in such a form that 17's position had
already been fixed within the corpus of the *Epodes*. In either case,
the result is that the last note of the *Satires* and the last note of the
Epodes is by design one and the same — Canidia.

Epodes 8 and 12 are companion pieces of savage physical and
moral αἰσχρολογία after the most unrestrained manner of Catullus
and the hellenistic poets. It is no doubt due to the coarseness of
subject matter that these artful poems have received very little
attention. I think, however, that wit and structure redeem and
elevate both pieces of fierce invective to something more than the
lowest level of humor and that within the conventional limitations
of good taste as much can easily be demonstrated.

The scholia of pseudo-Acron (on 12.1) tell us that Horace is
attacking the same woman in 8 and 12: *Eandem, quam supra,
adloquitur inpudentem in amorem suum.* If 8 and 12 do indeed deal
with a real woman and the same one, we have no way of knowing
who she is. Latsch believes strongly in the reality of the woman of
8: "Wer ist das Weib? Dass es eine Phantasiegestalt ist, kann ich
kaum glauben, ist doch der junge Horaz wie die Satiren beweisen,
stark realistisch."[44] Latsch again accepts the reality of the woman
of 12, but argues that lines 8.19-20:

> quod ut superbo provoces ab inguine
> ore allaborandum est tibi

must mean that Horace will have no traffic with this woman and,
therefore, that lines 12.15-16:

> Inachiam ter nocte potes, mihi semper ad unum
> mollis opus

must refer to a different woman. But *viris quid enervet meas* (8.2)
may very well suggest precisely what 12.15-16 say so bluntly.

---

[44] *Op. cit.* (above, n.II.3), 99-101.

While Zielinski[45] and Perret[46] tend to accept a single real person, Villeneuve is more cautious: "Si l'épode vise un personnage réel avons-nous affaire à la même femme que dans la huitième? En tout cas, le ton est semblable."[47] My own position is that the literalism of Latsch begs the question and that even within the realm of "starke Realität" it is itself open to dispute. What we must remember is that poems like 8 and 12 are of a traditional genre and as such they may merely be literary exercises appropriate to a book of *iambi*. Again, the absence of firm evidence and the vagaries of this kind of sordid relationship, if epodes 8 and 12 do portray a real and a single one, are such, especially in the poetic context of reality and imagination, that any interpretation is at best a guess. We simply do not know.

While both 8 and 12 viciously attack a woman, old, married, ugly, wealthy and oversexed, they are by no means carbon copies of each other. Both poems open on a crashing note of abuse cast in interrogative form:

> Rogare longo putidam te saeculo (?)[48]

and:

> Quid tibi vis, mulier nigris dignissima barris?

The method of 8 is then to state her question indirectly: *viris quid enervet meas* (8.2), and then to catalogue the old woman's anatomy part by part with appropriate offensive adjectives: *dens, frons, podex, pectus, mammae, femur* and *sura*, as an answer to her question. Horace's attention to her age is managed in two ways. The brutally direct *longo saeculo* is reinforced by the jarring tautology *vetus senectus*. Then as if to console her for her ugliness he says slyly (11-12):

[45] T. Zielinski, *Horace et la société romaine du temps d'Auguste* (Paris, 1938), 163.
[46] J. Perret, *Horace* (Paris, 1959), 63.
[47] *Op. cit.* (above, n.IV.23), 219.
[48] The correct punctuation of the sentence is interrogative. For the use of the infinitive (*te* guarantees the mood) to express indignation with interrogative punctuation compare 11.11-12: '*contrane lucrum nil valere candidum pauperis ingenium?*' See also Brunori, *op. cit.* (above, n.IV.17) 89, for parallels in other works.

> esto beata, funus atque imagines
> ducant triumphales tuum.

Notice the cruel collocation of *beata* and *funus*, as well as the implication: "You are so old that you are about to die — but your funeral will be a grand one!" Similarly, the consoling compliment on her *rotundiores bacae* rings false with the loaded *onusta*.[49] After a parting shot at the woman's literary and stoic pretensions (15-18), an obvious cover for her other interests, Horace concludes with the whiplash couplet (19-20).

The technique of 12 is considerably more sophisticated. Horace states the two points at issue clearly in line 3: *nec firmo iuveni neque naris obesae*. The former finds its explanation in *indomitam rabiem* (9), *tenta cubilia tectaque rumpit* (12), *mihi semper ad unum mollis opus* (15-16), *quaerenti taurum* and *te inertem* (16-17), and in *indomito inguine* (19). Though Horace admits that his *infirmitas* cannot satisfy her rabies, his *nares* in fact prohibit his trying.[50] The latter, the *naris obesae*, is deftly developed. Line 4 begins what the reader expects to be a simple body odor theme. Porphyrion (on 5) tells us that the *polypus ... naribus intellegendus*, and from Celsus we learn why this blemish, usually not visible to the lover's eye, is so objectionable. Of ulcerated nostrils, Celsus says: *Sin autem ea ulcera circa os sunt pluresque crustas et odorem foedum habent.*[51] The *sudor* (7) and *malus odor* (7-8) continue the body odor theme, but neatly interwoven is the phrase *vietis membris*, the first

---

[49] The fondness of Roman women for jewelry, especially pearls, was notorious. Ovid tells the Roman *puellae*, *de medicamine faciei* 17-22:

> At vestrae matres teneras peperere puellas:
> Vultis inaurata corpora veste tegi,
> Vultis odoratos positu variare capillos,
> Conspicuam gemmis vultis habere manum;
> Induitis collo lapides oriente petitos,
> Et quantos onus est aure tulisse duos.

[50] Porphyrion on 12.3: *nec firmo iuveni.* Hoc est, nec ualido qui sufficere libidini tuae possit. *neque naris obesae.* Hoc est neque occlusae naris, ut possim putorem corporis tui ferre.

[51] *De medicina* 6.8.2. Horace apparently found this ailment an especial blemish. Compare *Sat.* 1.3.38-40:

> illuc praevertamur, amatorem quod amicae
> turpia decipiunt caecum vitia, aut etiam ipsa haec
> delectant, veluti Balbinum polypus Hagnae.

hint in this section of old age and its accompanying uglines. These are not developed by an anatomical catalogue as was the case in epode 8. Instead, Horace uses *sudor* as the peg on which 9-11 hang: *neque illi | iam manet umida creta colorque | stercore fucatus crocodili*: no longer do her moist powder and complexion rouged with crocodile excrement remain. The suggestion is not merely that the mask is off, as Martial says of Galla: *nec tecum facies tua dormiat*,[52] but that the facade of paint argues an ugly base. The Augustan poets Tibullus and Propertius both voice disapproval of the use of cosmetics:

> quid [prodest] fuco splendente genas ornare?[53]

> an si caeruleo quaedam sua tempora fuco
> tinxerit, idcirco caerula forma bona est?[54]

Finally, Martial pinpoints the tendency of older women to compensate for nature by the overuse of cosmetic powder:[55]

> crassior in facie vetulae stat creta Fabullae

and the danger moisture presents to it:

> quam cretata timet Fabulla nimbum.

In *colorque stercore fucatus crocodili*, Horace has humorously blended two distinct cosmetic operations. *Neque color fucatus manet* simply means that her rouged complexion is running. The *stercore crocodili* is not completely an invented invective. Pliny tells us that the intestines of the land crocodile were much sought after as medication against facial blemishes: *crocodilea* would restore a pure complexion.[56] Its use is analogous to that of modern face creams, that is, it would be applied and worn in private. Horace substitutes *stercus* for *intestina* and deliberately

---

[52]   9.37.5.
[53]   Tibullus 1.8.11.
[54]   Propertius 2.18.31-32.
[55]   8.33.17, 2.41.11.
[56] *Historia naturalis* 28.28.108: alter [crocodilus] illi similis, multum infra magnitudine, in terra tantum odoratissimisque floribus vivit. ob id intestina eius diligenter exquiruntur iucundo nidore referta; crocodileam vocant. ... inlita quoque ex oleo cyprino molestias in facie nascentes tollit, ex aqua vero morbos omnes quorum natura serpit in facie, nitoremque reddit. lentigines tollit ac varos maculasque omnes. ...

confounds *crocodilea* with *fucus,* as if in fact her rouge were *crocodilea.*

The remarks of Scapha to Philematium nicely illuminate the scene Horace is portraying:

Quia ecastor mulier recte olet ubi nihil olet. / nam istae veteres, quae se unguentis uncitant, interpoles / vetulae, edentulae, quae vitia corporis fuco occulunt, / ubi sese sudor cum unguentis consociavit, ilico / itidem olent quasi quom una multa iura confudit coquos. / quid olant nescias, nisi id unum ut male olere intellegas.[57]

This much said by way of general comparison and contrast, a more detailed and individual analysis of each poem is necessary before we can reach precise conclusions on their structural relation. Giarratano's comments on the structure of epode 8 furnish a sound and convenient point of departure for our discussion:

L'epodo si divide in due parti equali. Nella prima è descritta l'oscena laidezza della vecchia. Si noti il τρίκωλον, che è uno caratteri particolari del periodo oraziano: 1. *dens ater,* 2. *vetus senectus,* 3. *turpis podex;* 1. *pectus et mammae putres,* 2. *venter mollis,* 3. *femur exile.* Nella seconda parte si mostra che ricchezza, nobiltà, dottrina vera o ostentata non bastano a risvegliare l'amore sensuale.[58]

The key phrase on which the implied answer to the question of lines 1-2 hangs is *longo putidam saeculo.* Lines 3-10 are in fact a bipartite catalogue of physical deformities concomitant with old age. The first half (3-6),[59] introduced by *cum* (followed by *et ... que*) and grammatically three clauses subordinate to *rogare,* lists three subjects each with its own verb. Giarratano takes the three

---

[57] Plautus, *Mostellaria* 273-278. J. Carcopino, *Daily Life in Ancient Rome* (tr. E. O. Lorimer, London, 1941) 168, pictures the normal duties of the matrona's *ornatrix*: "She had to remove her mistress's superfluous hair, and above all to 'paint' her: white on the brow and arms with chalk and white lead; red on cheeks and lips with ochre, *fucus,* or the lees of wine; black with ashes *(fuligo)* or powdered antimony on the eyebrows and round the eyes."

[58] Giarratano, *op. cit.* (above, n.III.6), 65. Kiessling-Heinze, *op. cit.* (above, n.III.6) 519-520: "1-10 Das Gegenbild einer detaillierenden Verherrlichung weiblicher Reize ...;" and "11-20 der zweite, dem ersten gleichlange Teil des Gedichts zählt her, worauf sich die Alte etwas zugute tut, und schliesst ebenda, wo der erste begann".

[59] O. Tescari, *I Carmi e gli Epodi* (Torino, 1936), 474, on 3-6: "Questi versi sono epesegetici di *putidam*", one argument against the structure of T. Plüss, *op. cit.,* (above, n.IV.19) 49; A 1-2; B I 3-6, 7-10, II 11-18; C 19-20.

subjects of the three verbs as a τρίκωλον, and grammatically this
is correct. Logically, it is open to two objections. First, *dens ater*
and *turpis podex* are not analogous to *vetus senectus*. Horace
notes two parts of the body; the abstract idea of old age does not
fit. The third member must be *frontem* (the object of the verb)
plowed with *rugis* or to express these as noun and adjective, *frons
rugosus*. Secondly, two general areas of the body are in question,
not three. *Dens* and *frontem* belong to the *facies*, while *podex* and
natis (which should be noted) belong to the *posterior*. One assumes
that there is a note of contrast present.

The second half (7-10) of the catalogue, like the first half (3-6),
is allotted four lines and likewise hangs on the peg of *putidam*, a
note which is struck again with *putres* at the end of line 7. In this
half, the anatomical list continues, but the view is not front and
rear; it is frontal descending from *pectus* and *mammae* to *venter*
(*sensu obsceno*) to *femur* and finally to *surae* (these last two form
a single item by virtue of *additum*, like two blocks of poorly
architectured masonry).[60] The whole catalogue is thus structured:

> I. *Facies* and *posterior* (3-6):
>   A. *dens ater* and *frons rugosus* (3-4)
>   B. *turpis podex* and *aridae nates* (5-6)
> II. Frontal view, descending (7-10):
>   A. *pectus et mammae putres* (7-8)
>   B. *venter mollis* (9)
>   C. *femur exile* and *tumentes surae* (9-10)

The second half of the epode (11-20) is more subtle and somewhat
differently structured. Not physical abuse, but pride and philo-
sophical pretense are now aired. *Esto beata*, "consider yourself
fortunate",[61] Horace orders (notice that lines 1 and 11 both begin

---

[60]   Porphyrion on 9-10: Ingeniosa descriptio. Nihil enim tam deforme est
quam crassiores pedes infra genua quam supra.
[61]   Giarratano, *op. cit.* (above, n.III.6), 66, translates *beata* as "ricca" and
adds: "come avevano inteso gli scoliasti". This is true for pseudo-Acron who
comments: Beatam eam pro divite dixit, as in *Odes* 2.4.13; and for Comm.
Cruq. who says *dives* and cites the same passage. But Porphyrion explains:
Placeas tibi licet generositate ac divitiis, inquit, dummodo deformitatem hanc
effugere non possis; the *beata* is meant to include both nobility and wealth.
In every other usage in the *Epodes* (2.1, 9.4, 16.41) the meaning of *beatus*
is not restricted to "wealthy" but is more general: "happy", "blessed", "fortunate".

with verbs) on two counts: your nobility and your wealth (11-14).
It takes little reading between the lines to understand that the lady
was vain about both and still less to see the ironic sarcasm in the
settings chosen: the *funus* suggests she is so old that death is near;
and the *onusta ambulet* suggests ostentatious display of her exces-
sive accessories. The whole is a parody of *consolatio*.

15-18 turn about books and philosophy, admitting several un-
flattering interpretations. Comm. Cruq. presents one (on 15):

Solita erat haec libros philosophorum etiam in lectis repositos habere
ad tegendam libidinem, ut adveniente amatore simularet se philosophiae
studere, non libidini.

And Horace asks whether those unlettered in that rigid[62] philosophy are in truth less firm.[63] The last two lines (19-20) are a whiplash
couplet furnishing a solution to the problem raised in 1-2, but
follow naturally and smoothly on *nervi* and *fascinum*.

The second major division (11-20) of the epode has, as indicated,
a structure akin but not identical with the first. Its first two sub-
divisions are each allotted four lines (11-14, 15-18) while the
whiplash ending occupies two (19-20) lines. The first major division
(1-10) has an almost identical linear allocation in reverse order:
two lines (1-2) + eight lines (3-10), the catalogue which is composed of two four-line units (3-6, 7-10). Noteworthy and appropriate to this pattern is the heavy ironic sarcasm in 7-10 (*sed incitat*,
etc.) and in 11-14 (*esto beata*), and the relationship of 1-2 to 19-20
as problem and solution.

The structure of epode 12 is clearly bipartite, each primary
division (1-13 and 14-26) having exactly thirteen lines. Horace,
upon receipt of letters and gifts, speak lines 1-13; 14-26 are the
directly quoted complaint of the *mulier* against Horace's inade-

---

[62]   *Epist*. 1.1.16-17:
         nunc agilis fio et mersor civilibus undis,
         virtutis verae custos rigidusque satelles
on the last two words of which Porphyrion comments: Bene rigidus, secundum
Stoicen.
[63]   This paraphrase gives the general sense of 17-18 which may be translated
in two ways. Villeneuve prints both, the less likely as a footnote, *op. cit.* (above,
n.IV.23), 214 note 3: "Pour n'avoir pas de lettres, les nerfs ont-ils moins de
raideur, le membre est-il languissant et de dimensions moindres? (le second
minus étant alors adjectif)."

quate response to her demands for affection. Thus the poem begins with Horace addressing the *mulier* and ends with her addressing him. As is the case with Canidia's speech in epode 17, the woman's speech confirms the worst that Horace speaking in his own person has said of her.

Lines 1-13 require careful consideration. Line 1 (*quid tibi vis, mulier*) alerts the reader that Horace is addressing some woman, and the next two lines continue the use of the second person singular (*mittis*). Presumably, at least the first half of the epode is to be spoken by Horace to the *mulier*. Line 3 furnishes the key to the development of 4-13, for the two points mentioned through litotes: *nec firmo iuveni neque naris obesae* (that is, Horace's infirmity and keen sense of smell) are the pegs on which the epexegetical 4-6 and 7-13 are chiastically hung. Horace's sensitivity to odor, the second point, is first exploited in lines 4-6, where he claims to be able to detect most keenly a polypus, goat or a sow (the number of items is characteristically three). These lines provide no grammatical clue to the person addressed, but on the basis of the very forms of 1-3 the reader naturally assumes that they are for the ears of the *mulier*.

Lines 7-13, however, upset this comfortable assumption. They exploit the first point of line 3, Horace's infirmity, though this is not at once apparent. The *sudor* and *odor* of 7-8 are deceptive, for they promise merely a continuation of the body odor theme. But the sense of lines 7-13 is: what sweat and what a foul odor arise when *pene soluto* she tries to sate her unrestrained rage *subando*, which attempt results only in her cosmetics running and the bed being broken, or when she tries to stir my pride with savage words. In 4-6 Horace claimed keen sensitivity to odor; in 7-13 the *mulier* is depicted as no mean source of odor. But the development of 7-13 depends less on the idea of odor than on that of Horace's infirmity, for *nec firmo* is explained not as a lack on his part but an excess of capacity on her part. The use of *sus* (6) and *subando* (11) furnishes an index to the problem: *sus* simply suggests odor, *subando* retains the note of odor but goes beyond that to the activities and requirements of that animal in heat. Porphyrion comments: *Subare proprie sues dicuntur, cum libidinantur; inde trans-*

latio est facta in caetera animalia. The net effect then is that while *sus* concretizes the theme of *odor*, it also serves to introduce the even stronger metaphor *subando*, which retains the note of *odor* and also concretizes the poem's second major theme *rabies*. It is precisely these requirements which the poet cannot meet, even if his olfactory sensitivity would permit a try.

We may now return to the problem of the addressee of 1-13. The pronoun of the third person *illi* (9) as well as the third singular verbs *properat* (9) and *rumpit* (12) of which *mulier* is subject mean that while Horace was addressing the woman in 1-3 and most probably in 4-6, she is at least in 7-13 conceived of in the third person.[64] The conclusion must be that 1-13 are a monologue by Horace in which his point of view shifts from questioning her (*absentem*) to recalling her actions.

The recollection of her actions of passion and words of scorn serves to introduce the second half of the epode, the directly quoted mulier's complaint (14-26), which we understand she uttered on one of the occasions portrayed in 7-13. In the first section (14-20) of seven lines (equal to the number of lines in 7-13) her side of the *nec firmo* question is aired. She contends that her rival, Inachia, enjoys the best of Horace's prowess and curses Lesbia[65] for suggesting Horace instead of the strong Amyntas. The unifying note of 14-20 is sexual prowess. 21-24 are a plaintive reproach to Horace's coldness grounded on her devotional generosity and employing the motifs of clothing and banquet, while 25-26 are a couplet summary of this her unhappy state in which the animal motif recalls that of line 1.

We may now complete our comparison of the structural techniques of these companion epodes. The results of our structural analyses may thus be indicated in terms of linear allocation:
epode 8:   20 = 10 (=2+8 [=4+4]) + 10 (=4+4+2)
epode 12:   26 = 13 (=6 [=3+3] +7) + 13 (=7+6 [=4+2])
First and most obvious is the bipartite structure of both epodes

---

[64] Tescari on 7-13, *op. cit.* (above, n.IV.59), 487: "Il poeta rivolge qui, in tono narrativo, il suo discorse al lettore."

[65] Possibly an *anus* like the mulier or a procuress. For a more imaginative account see L. Herrmann, "La carrière de Lesbia", *Latomus* 15 (1956), 308-313.

with a division into equal halves (10 and 13 lines, respectively). Second, the reader will notice that there is in both poems a chiastic arrangement of subordinate units so that 2 + 8 [=4+4] is paired with 4 + 4 + 2, and 6 [=3+3] + 7 is paired with 7 + 6 [=4+2], the numerical symmetry of epode 12 being less exact than that of epode 8.

With epodes 8 and 12 we have completed our discussion of companion pieces. It may be well to look at the distribution of these poems within the collection of the *Epodes*. Three of the four corresponding pairs of poems (5 and 17, 7 and 16, 8 and 12) are arranged in chiastic order, though they are not symmetrically distributed throughout the collection. One member of the Actium pair is placed at the beginning of each series of companion pieces. The complete pattern is: 1 and 9 in balanced order, with 5, 7 and 8 in chiastic arrangement with 12, 16 and 17:

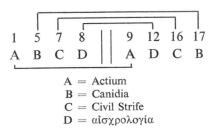

```
A = Actium
B = Canidia
C = Civil Strife
D = αἰσχρολογία
```

The anomalous arrangement of 1 and 9 calls attention to itself and warrants further consideration. It will be remembered that both 1 and 9 focus on Horace, Maecenas and Octavian, and have as their occasion the battle of Actium, the outstanding national event of the period of the composition of the *Epodes*. Poem 1 occupies the all-important initial position in the collection and 9 is at the very center of the seventeen poems. Thus numerically, Horace, Maecenas and Octavian are at the beginning and the heart of the collection with the remaining companion pieces arranged chiastically with reference to them. The verbal responsions of 1.1-4 and 9.1-4 have already been treated, but we may note again the parallels of Caesar (1.3) and Caesar (9.2), and the even more important duplication of (*amice*) Maecenas (1.4) and (*beate*) Maecenas (9.4), the addressee of both epodes.

A glance at the first book of *Satires*, published some years before the *Epodes*, will help to make clear Horace's technique. Port[66] takes satires 1 and 6 as dedications to Maecenas of the first and second halves of the book; notice the parallelism of Maecenas in the vocative case and in line 1 of each satire: *Qui fit, Maecenas* (1.1) and *Non quia, Maecenas* (6.1).[67] Fraenkel[68] correctly noted: "Here the vocatives can have only one meaning: the book as a whole and, by way of reminder, its second half are dedicated to Maecenas." Port further connected satires 6 and 10 as "Auseinandersetzungen mit Lucilius und Rechtfertigungen seiner eigenen Satirendichtung." Similarly, satires 5 and 9 correspond: "die beide die Erlebnisse auf einem zurückgelegten Weg erzählen." The foregoing establishes a partial structure of the book as follows:

$$
\begin{array}{cccccccccc}
 & \overline{} & & \overline{} & & & & & & \rceil \\
1 & 2 & 3 & 4 & 5 & | \, | & 6 & 7 & 8 & 9 \quad 10
\end{array}
$$

The division of the book is into halves with 1 and 6 in balance, and 4 and 5 chiastically arranged with 9 and 10.[69] The parallels of structure between the first book of *Satires* and the *Epodes* are striking: (1) the symmetrical placing of the vocative as an indication of dedication, (2) use of dedicatory poems in balanced order, (3) use of conspicuously corresponding poems in chiastic order, and (4) a division of the book into halves.[70]

[66] *Op. cit.* (above, n.I.3), 288-291.

[67] The technique of significantly placing the name Maecenas (vocative case) was fully exploited by Vergil, who names Maecenas only four times: *Georgics* 1.2, 2.41, 3.41, 4.2. The chiastic order is noteworthy.

[68] *Op. cit.* (above, n.IV.11), 101.

[69] A. Kiessling and R. Heinze, *Q. Horatius Flaccus. Satiren*[7] (Berlin, 1959) xxii, comment: "Die Zehnzahl der Gedichte und ihre Gliederung in zwei Hälften — denn die sechste Satire nimmt mit erneuter Anrede an Maecenas die Widmung gleichsam wieder auf — erinnert gewiss nicht zufällig an Virgils in Jahre 39 veröffentlichte bukolische Sammlung. Aber mit dieser Gliederung kreuzt sich eine andere inhaltlich begründete Gruppierung: 1-3 geben moralische Weisheit; 4-6 handeln vom Dichter selbst, den 4 als Schriftsteller, 5 auf Reisen im Kreise seiner Freunde, 6 als werdende und gewordene Persönlichkeit und in seinem täglichen Lebenswandel vorführt; die dritte Trias, 7-9, erzählt lustige Geschichten; jedesmal am Schlusse steht die für die Selbstschilderung des Dichters wichtigste Satire. Endlich gibt sich das 10. Gedicht als Epilog, dem schon als fertig gedachten Buche noch eben vor Torschluss angehängt."

[70] In the case of the *Epodes* the division into two parts must necessarily be

The use of the chiasmus as a structural device in the *Epodes* and the first book of *Satires* may very well be viewed as another of the influences of Vergil on Horace.[71] Whether or not one is prepared to accept *in toto* the "bucolic chapel" of Maury,[72] the pairing of eclogues 1 and 9 as "les épreuves de la terre", 2 and 8 as "les épreuves de l'amour", 3 and 7 as "la musique libératrice", and 4 and 6 as "les révélations surnaturelles" remains convincing.[73] The pairing

---

uneven because the total number of poems, seventeen, is uneven. Curiously, epodes 1-8 and 9-17 have approximately the same number of lines: 304 and 321. The tendency of Horace's earlier works to divide into halves is again evident in the second book of *Satires*. F. Boll, "Die Anordnung im zweiten Buch von Horaz' Satiren", *Hermes* 48 (1913) 143-145, has conclusively argued the following arrangement:

1. Hälfte		2. Hälfte
1	Konsultation	5
2	Ländliches Genügen	6
3	Saturnalienpredigt	7
4	Gastrosophie	8

This arrangement has become standard. See Port, *op. cit.* (above, n.I.3), 291; Perret, *op. cit.* (above, n.IV.46), 245; O. Weinreich, *Römische Satiren* (Zürich, 1949), liii; Kiesling-Heinze, *op. cit.* (above, n.IV.69), xxiii; and Wili, *op. cit.* (above, n.IV.15) 72-73. E. Fraenkel, "Carattere della poesia augustea", *Maia* 1 (1948), 245-264, accepted Boll's arrangement without reservation; in his *Horace* (above, n.IV.11), 137, Fraenkel is more cautious: "Yet even if we reserve judgment on the completeness of the parallelism we may admit that the division of the book into two roughly symmetrical parts is marked by several corresponding features in the first and in the second half."

[71] For a summary and analysis of the influence of Horace and Vergil upon one another with emphasis on national themes see G. E. Duckworth, *"Animae Dimidium Meae*: Two Poets of Rome", *TAPA* 87 (1956), 281-316.

[72] P. Maury, "Le secret de Virgile et l'architecture des Bucoliques", *Lettres d'Humanité* 3 (1944), 71-147.

[73] For bibliography on the structure of the *Eclogues* see G. E. Duckworth, "Recent Work on Vergil (1940-1956), IV-V", *CW* 51 (1958), 123-128. See also P. Miniconi, "Les proportions mathématiques dans l'Énéide", *Latomus* 22 (1963), 263-273, who accepts Maury's impressive mathematical symmetries. E. A. Hahn, "The Characters in the Eclogues", *TAPA* 75 (1944) 196-241, argues that in addition to the accepted theory of the arrangement of odd-numbered eclogues as dialogues and even-numbered ones as monologues, another arrangement is operative: three triads plus a single eclogue "which completes and concludes the whole". The first (1, 2 and 3) and the third (7, 8 and 9) triads depict shepherds with realism; the second triad (4, 5 and 6) treats "more cosmic themes". In eclogue 10 the gods of the second triad and the shepherds of the first and third triads "freely mingle". This arrangement is not so different from Maury's as seems at first sight, for Miss Hahn notes within her

of eclogues 5 and 10: "Gallus est l'antithèse et l'antipode de Daphnis: tous les deux poètes et amoureux" completes the symmetry. Diagrammed less mystically than Maury has them, the *Eclogues* furnish this scheme:

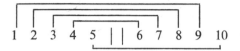

The division of the book is into halves with 1, 2, 3 and 4 arranged chiastically with 6, 7, 8 and 9. 5 and 10 are placed in balance, each at the end of a series of four eclogues. Aside from chiastic arrangement, the *Eclogues* share with the first book of *Satires* and the *Epodes* a division into halves. In the case of the first book of *Satires* and the *Epodes* balance was achieved by placing dedicatory poems at the beginning of each half of the work; in the *Eclogues* we have no dedicatory poems, instead balance is achieved by pairing 5 and 10 at the end of each half of the work.

Of the epodes which are usually classified as invectives, we have already considered 5, 8, 12 and 17. There remain 4, 6 and 10. 4 launches a two-directional attack against an unnamed upstart *tribunus militum*. Once a slave and scourged with Spanish ropes, Horace tells him, he now struts the Via Sacra proud of his wealth and ostentatious toga. A chorus of Roman passers-by echoes Horace's complaint, indignantly recalling that the upstart, once whipped to the loathing of the *praeco*, now drawn by Gallic ponies rides the Appian Way. 6 directs its attack against an unnamed opponent. This time the offense is that of cowardly harassing the innocent. Horace, comparing himself first to a sheep dog and then to a bull with ready horns, announces that, when attacked with *atro dente*, he will counterattack.[74]

---

structure a "one-to-one correspondence in inverse order" (= chiasmus): eclogues 3 and 7, 2 and 8, 1 and 9, and hence the first and the third triads are chiastically arranged. For another division of the *Eclogues* (into halves) see C. Becker, "Vergils Eklogenbuch", *Hermes* 83 (1955), 341-349.

[74] It might be appropriate to note in connection with epode 6 that after a careful reading of L. Herrmann's *Horace. Épodes* (Berchem-Bruxelles, 1953) I have decided to omit from consideration his reconstruction of the *Epodes* of Horace. The following will indicate the reasons for this decision. Herrmann

Zielinski once aptly observed, "Pourquoi le poète s'est-il imposé cette régularité gênante, que le lecteur n'aperçoit qu'après un compte pénible? Nous ne pouvons le dire, mais puisqu'elle est évidente, il faut bien la reconnaître."[75] I do not here intend to attempt to answer Zielinski's question. Rather, I wish to demonstrate just how intricate Horace's structures can be. In both epode 4 and epode 6 the major structural pattern is really clear enough to follow with only modest assistance. However, both poems, when carefully examined, reveal the subtle employment of a secondary structure of balance, echo and contrast to the extent that even the seasoned reader of Horace is left somewhat bewildered at the poet's architectural control. Let us, taking epodes 4 and 6, see just how Horace employs this technique of the double structure.

Epode 4 is a strange and deceptive composition. If one is prepar-

---

says, 7: "Nous montrerons d'abord que ces poèmes totalisaient primitivement un nombre de vers multiple de 18." Herrmann, according to his "règle des dix-huit vers", dismisses epode 13 ("une ode égarée", "... glissé dans le recueil des poèmes iambiques ...") from the collection, adds a newly composed verse to epode 17 (41bis ‹sonaberisque: "*Tu pudica, tu proba*"› The apparatus reads: 41bis vers., versu 40 nisus, refeci) to give the poem an even number of lines (81 lines become 82), dislodges epode 6 from its habitat between epodes 5 and 7 and relocates it after epode 9, and finally he adds to epode 6 *Catalepton* 13 which he terms VIbis. I pass over Herrmann's many gratuitous transpositions of lines.

[75]   T. Zielinski, "L'envoûtement de la sorcière chez Horace." *Mélanges offerts à O. Navarre par ses élèves et ses amis* (Toulouse, 1935) 439-451. His immediate reference was to the structural symmetry of epode 5:

      I. la plainte d'un petit garcon (1-10)
     II. les quatres sorcières à l'œuvre (11-46)
    III. imprécation de Canidie (47-82)
    IV. imprécation thyestéenes (83-102)

E. Turolla, *I Giambi* (Torino, 1957), 36, accepts the same division but accents the dramatic form of the piece:

    Prologo (1-10)
     I. Parte. Le maliarde all'opera (11-46)
    II. Parte. Canidia e Varo (47-82)
    Epilogo. La maledizione (83-102)

It has further been observed time and again that the numerical division: $10+36+36+20$ presents a symmetry deliberate on the author's part but difficult for the reader to perceive without resorting to a counting of lines. The puer's opening plea occupies ten lines while his concluding curse takes twenty, exactly double. For the witches' part, their δρώμενα occupy thirty-six lines while Canidia's λεγόμενα take an equal thirty-six.

ed to believe that Horace was himself a Roman knight,[76] and since in any case we know that he was a *tribunus militum*,[77] the attack on an ex-slave now become a knight and a military tribune is strange. It is all well and good to argue that Horace is attacking the contradiction of the man's lawless and servile past and his current pretensions, but change of civic status and the military position are too coincidental to make the reader altogether comfortable with the person of Horace launching the attack.

Structurally, the epode is deceptive, for it falls into two easily discernible and equal parts. In lines 1-10 Horace addresses his indignation to the upstart and in lines 11-20 a chorus[78] of Roman men-on-the-street voice the same but to one another. In 1-2, Horace launches the frontal attack with a comparison whose point is reinforced by the parallelism of word order and placement: *lupis et agnis ... obtigit* (1) and *tecum mihi ... est* (2). The next two lines (3-4) give the first objection Horace has and it is only a hint of what is to come. The person in question is a slave and a lawless one, for he has been scourged and chained. 5-6 tell us more; the slave is in fact an ex-slave who struts about arrogant in his (newly acquired) wealth, but Horace is quick to remind him that prosperity cannot change his servile stock. For confirmation, the poet invites our *parvenu* to observe the *liberrima indignatio* of the Roman men-on-the-street evoked by his pompous "pacing off" of the Via Sacra dressed in an extravagantly full toga (7-10).

II then allows the chorus of Romans to echo Horace's objections. We first hear them complain of the man's lawless servile status (11-12) as contrasted with his present wealth (13) and his ostentatious frequenting of the Appian Way with his expensive ponies (14).[79] And that is not all, for he has also become a knight, a

[76] See L. R. Taylor, "Horace's Equestrian Career", *AJP* 46 (1925), 161-169, whose arguments are substantial. The question was again reviewed by A. Noirfalise, "Horace, Chevalier Romain", *LEC* 18 (1950), 16-21, who concludes: "... notre poète fut et resta chevalier."
[77] *Sat.* 1.6.48.
[78] Fraenkel (above, n.IV.11), 58: "With a felicitous stroke he concludes the poem by making us listen to the comments of the populus. Exactly half of the epode is occupied by the talk of the chorus." The bipartite division is also noted by Giarratano (above, III, n.6), 42.
[79] As Porphyrion's note suggests, we are taking the parvenu's route from his

magnus (ironic) *eques*, who sits in the first row at the theatre. Surely Otho's law, which reserved the first fourteen rows for the knights, was passed with no expectation of a freedman attaining the status of knight.[80] The *Othone contempto* then concludes this section with a note of the defiance of the law, the same as the first objection raised by Horace (3-4) and the first raised by the chorus (11-12).

Lines 17-20 I consider a political addendum (not in the sense Kumaniecki understands)[81] spoken by the chorus and supplying an element absent but not unprepared for in 1-10 and especially in 11-16. That the Romans at any time should have to endure such an upstart is bad enough, but to endure him as a military tribune at a time when the nation is expending a full scale (*tot* ora navium *gravi* rostrata duci *pondere*) effort against Sextus Pompey's brigands (lawlessness) and servile (slavery) band is intolerable. The political note is not only relevant because of the upstart's background but because the impassioned *hoc, hoc tribuno militum* also harkens back to lines 15-16 where the *eques* was seated somewhere in the first fourteen rows as we understand from *primis*. Now the office of the military tribune entitles him to even the first privileged position of the equestrian order, a seat in the first two rows of the fourteen rows reserved for knights.

We may now turn to the suggestion that the poem's simple dual division is deceptive. The division of 1-10 and 11-20 is undeniable, but there is a haunting, if incomplete, parallelism which oversteps the given boundary by two lines (9-10):

---

estate to Rome: Proprie, quia Falerni agri meminerat, quo scilicet Appia necesse est ire.

[80] See C. G. Cobet, "Ad leg. 1. D. *ad legem Iuliam de vi privata*. Lex Roscia. Lex Iulia theatralis", *Mnemosyne* 10 (1861), 337-342, and G. Rotondi, *Leges publicae populi Romani* (Milano, 1912), 374-375.

[81] C. F. Kumaniecki, "De epodis quibusdam Horatianis", *Commentationes Horatianae* (Cracoviae, 1935), 139-157, argues that the last four lines (17-20) are spoken not by the Roman citizens but by Horace himself. Kumaniecki would date the epode in 39 B.C. after the peace treaty when a new conflict was at hand, and sees 17-20 as another Horatian protest against the resumption of war: "Quod tamen ep. VII pathetice verbisque horrore perfusis exposuit, id ep. IV tamquam ἐν παρέργῳ leviter indicavit." I follow the standard dating (between 38 and 36) and assignment of lines to the Romans.

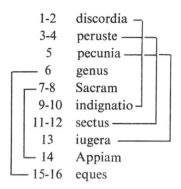

As the diagram indicates, the discord between Horace and the
upstart in 1-2 is paralleled by the indignation of the passers-by for
the upstart in 9-10. The burning lashes of 3-4 are matched by the
cutting ones of 11-12. Money (5) and land (13) are singled out as
the particulars of wealth. The balanced order thus far achieved
now varies with chiasmus, for the humble slave origin (6) is contrasted with the newly acquired equestrian title (15-16), and the
locale ranges from the Sacred Way (7) to the Appian Way (14).

For clarity, the diagram merely indicates the key words of the
relationship, but the parallels of both sense and language are
considerably wider. For example, *Hibericis peruste funibus* (3) is
paired with the *sectus flagellis triumviralibus* (11), so that even the
parts of speech reflect the relationship. In 1-2 the last two words
are *discordia est*; in 9-10 the last word is *indignatio*. Lines 5-7
stressed strutting and pacing off (*ambules ... metiente*), while lines
13-14 stress plowing the earth and pressing it down (*arat ... terit*),
the whole culminating in the sedentary imagery of 15-16 (*sedilibus*,
first word in 15; *sedet*, last word in 16). Unit of measure (*bis trium
ulnarum*) in line 8 is again taken up in line 13 (*mille*). Finally,
the transition from 7-8 to 9-10 is smoothened by the visuals, *vides*
and *ora vertat*.

Further parallels admissible are: two proper adjectives *Hibericis*
and *Sacram* in 1-10 with two proper adjectives *Falerni* and *Appiam*
in 11-20. Lines 1-6 are declarative statements with 7-10 a question;
lines 11-16 are a declarative statement with 17-20 a question.

Finally, the *praeconis fastidium* in 11 is ironically distorted to *Othone contempto* in 16.

The primary division of epode 6 is based on the change from the metaphorical image of a dog to that of a bull. In the first case (1-10), both Horace and the defamer are pictured as dogs, in the second (11-16), Horace is likened to a bull and then to a child,[82] while the defamer is no longer conceived of metaphorically. Lines 1-4 are composed of two complementary questions.[83] The first accuses the *canis* of attacking the harmless wayfarers,[84] while cowardly avoiding the wolf; and the second challenges him to attack Horace, who unlike the *immerentes hospites* is prepared to bite back.

As Buchheit[85] rightly points out *remorsurum* is the "Stichwort" on which the following lines hang, as well as the rest of the poem. The metaphor initiated in lines 1-4 is exploited to Horace's satisfaction in 5-10 and then discarded in favor of another. In 5-8, Horace is thinking of himself not only as the Molossian or Laconian hound who protects the flock by defensively opposing the aggressor wolf, but also as the hunting dog[86] whose function goes beyond that of driving off the intruder to offensively seeking out any sort of beast.[87] In contrast to this, the defamer of 9-10 is still portrayed only as the supposed protector of the flock who, when he has filled the grove with his barking, is pacified by scraps which the intimidated wayfarer is compelled to throw him. When 9-10 are so understood,[88] they not only stand in contrast to 5-8, but also

---

[82] The contrast of bull and child is jarring, though less so after the transition to the human by *gener* (13) and *hostis* (14).

[83] The interrogative form is resumed only in the last two verses (15-16), so that the poem begins and ends with a question.

[84] For this translation of *hospites* see Shorey-Laing, *Horace. Odes and Epodes* (Chicago, 1919), 493.

[85] V. Buchheit, "Horazens programmatische Epode (VI)", *Gymnasium* 68 (1961), 520-526.

[86] Molossian and Laconian dogs are both guardians of the flock and hunting dogs according to Vergil, *Georgics* 3.404-413.

[87] *Quaecumque fera [bestia]* translates as "whatever wild beast". But *ferus* (see *TLL* 6.1.602-603) is employed frequently enough with *canis* or *homo* so as not to exclude and indeed to suggest the defamer as an appropriate object of pursuit.

[88] Comm. Cruq.: Id est, tu cum tumidus et minitans inveheris in aliquem,

reflect back to lines 1-4. The *vexatio* (1) is managed by launching *inanis minas* (3) and is metaphorically portrayed as filling the *nemus* with *timenda voce*.

The second half of the epode (11-16), though it begins with the second person singular *cave*, allows the defamer to fall into the background and concentrates its attention on the opposition generalized, as the *in malos* (11) and the *si quis* (15) suggest, and Lycambes (13) and Bupalus (14) personify. The change of opponent goes hand in hand with the change of metaphor from dog to bull. Whereas in 1-10 Horace and the defamer were dog and dog, in 11-16 Horace no longer employs a metaphor for the opposition, and likens himself to a ready bull as contrasted with a helpless child.

In the course of his discussion of this piece as Horace's programmatic epode, Buchheit calls our attention to the verbal parallels and echoes, many of which are already sporadically noted by the commentators. Most notable is the paralellism of 5-8 with 11-14: *nam qualis aut ... aut* and *namque ... qualis ... aut*. Actually, the parellelism admits extension: *nam qualis aut Molossus aut fulvus Lacon* and *namque ... qualis ... spretus ... gener aut acer hostis*. That the two dogs are paralleled by the two poets is clear enough, but *fulvus*, by the figure ἀπὸ κοινοῦ,[89] qualifies both *Lacon* and *Molossus* and thereby creates a subtle if less precise parallel with *spretus* and *acer*. In other words, all four nouns are qualified. Again, 3-4 may be compared with 15-16. Buchheit notes *petis* (4) and *petiverit* (15) but the responsion is wider (*quin ..., si, ...*

---

expectas ut accepta pecunia desinas maledicere. It is unnecessary and confusing to understand with Kiessling-Heinze (above, n.III.6), 515, or with Giarratano (above, n.III.6), 59, "il ladro getta l'offa". The *hospites* of line 1 are being menaced.

[89] The figure was noted by Giarratano (above, n.III.6), 59, who refers the reader to p. 344 of F. Koldewey, "Figura ἀπὸ κοινοῦ bei Catull, Tibull, Properz und Horaz", *ZG* 31 (1877) 337-358, where only the use of the Horatian verb ἀπὸ κοινοῦ is discussed. The passage (6.5) is not anywhere mentioned by Koldewey, nor in the more recent study of J. Grimm, *The Construction* ΑΠΟ ΚΟΙΝΟΥ *in the Works of Horace* (Philadelphia 1928), outside of whose scope it falls. At any rate, Giarratano's observation is solid; and the construction is noted by H. D. Naylor (above, n.IV.17), 249. *Feris alitibus atque canibus* (17.11-12) furnishes one of many analogies.

me ... petis and *an si ... me petiverit*) and hence accents the contrast of *remorsurum* (4) with *inultus flebo* (16).

Thus far a tidy secondary structure of echo and parallel emerges. Buchheit by connecting 1-2 and 9-10 suggests a balance which when joined with the chiastic disposition indicated completes the structure:

$$
\begin{array}{l}
1\text{-}2 \\
3\text{-}4 \\
5\text{-}8 \\
9\text{-}10 \\
11\text{-}14 \\
15\text{-}16
\end{array}
$$

Here, the Latin needs to be examined carefully:

> Quid immerentis hospites vexas canis
> ignavus adversum lupos? (1-2)

> quin huc inanis, si potes, vertis minas,
> et me remorsurum petis? (3-4)

> tu cum timenda voce complesti nemus,
> proiectum odoraris cibum. (9-10)

We have already noted that *vexatio* (1) is accomplished by launching *inanis minas* (3). *Timenda voce* (9) as a metaphor further clarifies both *vexas* and *inanis minas*. To be sure, the ear associates more immediately and closely *minas* with *voce* as the barking of a dog with the voiced threats of men, but the parties and locale concerned in 1-2 are the same in 9-10: the *canis* and the *hospites* at the *nemus*. In so far as a relationship of the dimeter verses may be spoken of, *proiectum odoraris cibum* (10) may be associated with *ignavus adversum lupos* (2), through the idea of a want of aggressiveness, whereas *me remorsurum petis* (4) is quite the contrary.

Finally, the conflict relationship of the wayfarers and Horace with the opposition supports the validity of an ancillary structure:

total lines	lines			total lines	lines
2	1-2	opposition vs. wayfarers———opposition vs. wayfarers	9-10	2
2	3-4	opposition vs. Horace (and the reverse)	Horace vs. opposition	11-14	4
4	5-8	Horace vs. opposition	opposition vs. Horace (and the reverse)	15-16	2

Key words are: *vexas hospites* (1-2) and *tu complesti nemus* (9-10); *vertis minas, me remorsurum petis* (3-4) and *quis me petiverit, inultus flebo* (15-16); *agam quaecumque fera* (5-8) and *in malos tollo cornua* (11-14).

As I said in the beginning of this discussion, my purpose was to demonstrate in two instances Horace's technique of the double structure, rather than to discuss the aesthetics behind it. To be sure, the double structure, without the reader's awareness of it, makes the poem what it is to the extent that form can be said to participate in meaning. Once, however, the reader has taken the trouble to work out and is consciously aware of the patterns and variations, he has come to grips with the poetry on still another level. Perhaps an example in miniature of Horace's architectural control will best allow each reader to judge why he takes delight in the conscious perception of pattern and variation (*Odes.* 14.19-20):

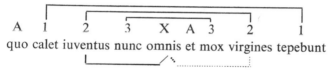

Epode 10, like epodes 4 and 6, addresses itself to a male opponent; this time, however, he is named. Maevius' only offense seems to be body odor (10.1-2):

> Mala soluta navis exit alite,
> ferens olentem Maevium

but that he merits shipwreck as an enemy of both Vergil and Horace we know from elsewhere. In this reverse *propempticon inimico poetae*, Horace calls upon winds, stars and seas to collaborate in the destruction of Maevius, in gratitude for which a sportive goat and a lamb shall be sacrificed to the *Tempestates*.[90]

We have already noticed the distribution of the companion pieces of invective (5 and 17, 8 and 12) directed against women. The combined distribution of invectives against men (4, 6 and 10) and invectives against women (5, 8, 12 and 17) appears to be

[90] For a fuller discussion of this poem see my "The Architecture of Horace's Tenth Epode", *Eranos* 63 (1966), 158-166.

designed to alternate the sex of the person attacked in so far as the
basic metrical arrangement permits (M = male, F = female):

4	5	6	8	10	12	17
M	F	M	F	M	F	F

The pattern of alternation would have been more satisfying and
complete if arranged F M F M F M F, with the three male invectives interspersed among the four female invectives. The difficulty
with such an arrangement is metrical, for 4, 6 and 10 are couplets
of iambic trimeter and dimeter and hence are metrically restricted
to positions in the first metrical group (1-10). Epodes 12 and 17,
therefore, cannot have an alternating male invective between them.
Instead, the arrangement as we have it is MF three times with
17 (F) repeating the feminine note.

The bulk (1-66) of epode 2 extolls the blessings of country life.
After an idyllic treatment of the rustic activities suited to the
various seasons (9-36), Horace devotes a long passage (45-60) to the
praise of simple country fare:[91]

> claudensque textis cratibus laetum pecus
>   distenta siccet ubera,
> et horna dulci vina promens dolio
>   dapes inemptas apparet;
> non me Lucrina iuverint conchylia
>   magisve rhombus aut scari,
> si quos Eois intonata fluctibus
>   hiems ad hoc vertat mare,
> non Afra avis descendat in ventrem meum,
>   non attagen Ionicus
> iucundior, quam lecta de pinguissimis
>   oliva ramis arborum
> aut herba lapathi prata amantis et gravi
>   malvae salubres corpori,
> vel agna festis caesa Terminalibus
>   vel haedus ereptus lupo.

Epode 3, taking up the theme of simple country fare, singles out
garlic as the object of a mock heroic invective. Line 4 reminds us
that we are still in the realm of the country:

> o dura messorum ilia!

[91]   See my "Horace, *Epod.* 2.49-60", *CB* 41 (1965), 62-63, on the structural
symmetry of this epode.

Like epode 2, epode 3 is structured with exceeding care, so much so that to pass over the structure-content relationship is to experience only a fraction — a small one — of the poem.[92] Consider the following structural outline of epode 3:

I. Parricide and his punishment (1-4):
Let the parricide eat garlic (which only reapers can stomach) more toxic than hemlock.
II. Identification of the cause of Horace's illness (5-18):
    A. Two possibilities (5-8):
        The question: What sort of poison burns my innards? (5)
        1st possibility: Has viper's blood gotten into the food? (6-7)
        2nd possibility: Has Canidia tampered with the food? (7-8)
    B. Two identifications (9-14):
        Introduction to the Medea myth (9-10)
        1st identification: With this Medea anointed Jason (11-12)
        2nd identification: With this Medea anointed Creusa's gifts (13)
        Conclusion to the Medea myth (14)
    C. Two rejected comparisons (15-18):
        1st comparison: Not so great is the heat of the star over Apulia (15-16)
        2nd comparison: Not more hotly did the gift burn on Heracles 17-18)
III. Maecenas and his punishment (19-22):
Playful Maecenas, if ever you desire such a thing, I pray that your girl refuse you her charms.

Probably the most artful structure to be found in any of the epodes is that of epode 3. Over-all the poem invites a neat tripartite structure: 1-4, 5-18, 19-22.[93] I treats the parricide and his punishment, II seeks to identify the cause of Horace's illness, and III deals with Maecenas and his punishment. The tone and intent of epode 3 cannot be mistaken. The content and structure of the

---

[92] The following remarks are essentially the same as those in my "La structure de la troisième Épode d'Horace", *LEC* 33 (1965), 412-417.
[93] So Plüss (above, n.IV.19), 16-17. But my division of 5-18 differs from those of Plüss, Giarratano (above, n.III.6), 38, and Fraenkel (above, n.IV.11), 68.

first sentence are a calculated parody of Roman *leges* into which a note of Greek law (*cicuta*) is intruded:[94]

> Parentis olim si quis impia manu
>   senile guttur fregerit,
> edit cicutis alium nocentius.

The sentence begins with a *si quis* clause in the future perfect indicative which expresses the prohibited action (*parentis guttur fregerit*) and concludes with a main clause ordering the attached penalty (*edit alium*). The fragmentary remains of Roman Law from the first century B.C. do not furnish an exact parallel but the *Codex Justinianus* 9.17 (*de his qui parentes vel liberos occiderunt*) does:

> Si quis parentis ... fata properaverit, ... insutus culleo et inter eius ferales angustias comprehensus serpentium contuberniis misceatur et ... vel in vicinum mare vel in amnem proiciatur ...[95]

---

[94]   For the serious aspects of Horace and Roman Law see E. Henriot, *Mœurs juridiques et judiciaires de l'ancienne Rome d'après les poètes latins* (Paris, 1865) who, 2.182, somewhat naïvely refers to the question of parricide in Horace as "mentionné ... à titre de supposition"; E. Costa, *Il diritto nei poeti di Roma* (Bologna, 1898); F. Stella Maranca, "Per lo studio del diritto romano nell'opera di Orazio", *Archivio giuridico "Filippo Serafini"*, 13 (1935), 31-88; "Introduzione allo studio del Diritto Romano nell'opera di Orazio", *Historia* 9 (1935), 3-21, 369-400, 531-573; "Orazio e la legislazione romana", *Conferenze Oraziane* (Milan, 1936), 43-66; A. F. Murison, "The Law in the Latin Poets", *Atti del congresso internazionale di Diritto Romano* (Pavia, 1935), 2.609-639, who assures us that "... the Roman poets were sound in their law, as far as their law went"; and J. Moseley, "Did Horace Study Law?" *TAPA* 66 (1935), xxix, who suggests that from the influence of legal language and procedure upon Horace's style and thinking we may conclude that he studied law with particular favor or perhaps with the intention of entering that profession.
[95]   See also Festus, *de significatione verborum*, *s.v. parrici*, and *Digesta* 48.9.1 (*de lege Pompeia de parricidiis*). Horace may have had the latter (enacted in 55 or 52 B.C.) in mind when writing this epode: Lege Pompeia de parricidiis cavetur, ut, si quis patrem ... occiderit ... ut poena ea teneatur, quae est legis Corneliae de sicariis. Aristophanes, *Birds* 1072-1075, employs the technique of legal parody with reference to ψηφίσματα:

> τῇδε μέντοι θἠμέρᾳ μάλιστ᾽ ἐπαναγορεύεται,
> ἢν ἀποκτείνῃ τις ὑμῶν Διαγόραν τὸν Μήλιον,
> λαμβάνειν τάλαντον, ἤν τε τῶν τυράννων τινα
> τῶν τεθνηκότων ἀποκτείνῃ, τάλαντον λαμβάνειν.

On this day a special proclamation is made: If anyone of you kills Diagoras the Melian, he shall receive a reward of one talent; if anyone kills any of the tyrants already long dead, he too shall receive a reward of one talent.

The playfully humorous tone of the epode continues with out-
landish comparisons of garlic with Canidia's poisons, the drugs of
Medea, the heat of Apulia and the ointment which burned Heracles.
The *iocose* of line 20 reminds us that the bathetic prayer Horace
utters against his friend and host Maecenas is not to be taken
seriously (19-22):

> at si quid umquam tale concupiveris,
>   iocose Maecenas, precor
> manum puella savio opponat tuo,
>   extrema et in sponda cubet.

But the effectiveness of the poem's last four lines is only fully
appreciated when their content[96] as well as their form are compared
with those of the first three lines. The form of lines 1-3 was *si quis*
with the future perfect indicative in the third person singular
followed by the jussive subjunctive in the third person singular.
This form is largely retained but also altered, personalized and
considerably softened in lines 19-22. We have *si quid* and *umquam*
(= *olim* of line 1) with the future perfect indicative (*concupiveris*)
in the second person singular followed by the subjunctive in the
third person singular, this time not a jussive but dependent upon
precor,[97] "I pray that." The tone of *precor* as opposed to the
jussive is that of a prayer as opposed to that of a command. The
force in English is:

If anyone ever shall have broken with impius hand the aged neck of his
parent, let him eat garlic more toxic than hemlock.

But if, playful Maecenas, you ever shall have desired anything similar,
I pray that your girl place her hand to your kiss and sleep at the far
edge of the couch.

The culpable party of 1-4 is the parricide, any parricide and not a
specific one, while the culpable party of 19-22 is specified, no one
but Maecenas. The progression then is from the general to the
specific.

---

[96] Fraenkel (above, n.IV.11), 69, correctly observes: "The petty anticlimax
at the end (21 f.) is in harmony with the mocking spirit of the poem; the touch
is so light that the apparent curse sounds like an affectionate compliment to
Maecenas."
[97] The poetic use of *precor* followed by the subjunctive without *ut* is the rule
in Horace. See *Odes* 1.2.30, 1.3.7, 1.31.18.

quid hoc veneni saevit in praecordiis?
    num viperinus his cruor
incoctus herbis me fefellit, an malas
    Canidia tractavit dapes?
ut Argonautas praeter omnis candidum
    Medea mirata est ducem,
ignota tauris illigaturum iuga
    perunxit hoc Iasonem;
hoc delibutis ulta donis paelicem
    serpente fugit alite.
nec tantus umquam siderum insedit vapor
    siticulosae Apuliae,
nec munus umeris efficacis Herculis
    inarsit aestuosius.

The basic tripartite structure of the epode is further reflected in the
structure of II as A two possibilities, B two identifications, and
C two rejected comparisons. Syntactically, A begins with a
question (*quid hoc*) which introduces the rest of A as well as B and
C. Horace asks what is burning his innards,[98] and as a first
response he poses a double question: *num ... fefellit, an ... tractavit?*
containing two possibilities: viper's blood or the work of Canidia?
5-8 then are organized around the form of a question: *quid* (5), *num*
(6) and *an* (7). B (9-14) offers definite answers and tells a tale.
9-10 recall for us the initial meeting of Jason and Medea and how
the princess fell in love at first sight with the leader of the Argonaut
expedition. 11-13 then take two episodes from their story of love
and magic. Horace is sure that the substance with which (*hoc* at 12)
she anointed Jason and with which (*hoc* at 13) she anointed Creusa's
gifts is in fact the same substance which is causing his burning
sensation — the poet makes two identifications. In the last line (14)
of B, Medea flees on a winged serpent, the conclusion to the Medea
myth complementing the first two lines of B (9-10), the introduction
to the myth. Both quite properly frame the two occasions of
magic. C, the third and the last unit of II, rejects two comparisons,

---

[98]   A. Y. Campbell, *Horace. Odes and Epodes*[2] (Liverpool, 1953), 151: "The
first four lines of the piece are H,'s comment after he has realized that his
trouble is due to having eaten garlic. But in 5-8 he is still speculating about
the cause. I take it then that 5-18 are (so to speak) dramatic ... the victim's
first reactions to his symptoms; he is supposed to be repeating these indignantly
to Maecenas. I have therefore placed 5-18 within inverted commas."

each of which is allotted two lines: not so great is the heat of the Star (15-16), not more hotly does the gift burn (17-18). The structure is guaranteed by the use of *nec* as the first word of 15 and a second *nec* as the first word of 17.[99]

The comment of Fraenkel[100] that, "Pre-eminence is given to the *venena Colcha*: the story of Medea's sorcery (9-14) fills six lines; to make the story still more conspicuous it is placed exactly in the center of the poem" suggests further observations on linear allocation in epode 3. The six lines 9-14 are the central focus of 5-18 as well as of the entire poem. Horace has chosen to devote four lines (5-8) to two possibilities, six lines to Medea's two drugs, and finally four lines (15-18) to the two comparisons. The linear allocation of II is then $4 + 6 + 4$. The entire poem is: $4 + 14$ ($=4+6+4$) $+ 4$ which suggests the term "recessed panel".

The choice and arrangement of the six items of II also warrant further comment. In II A, the viper's blood and Canidia (real person or type character) are drawn from real life; in II B, the two drugs are drawn from myth; in II C, the star over Apulia is drawn

---

[99] P. Colmant, "Horace, *Épode* III", *LEC* 25 (1957), 107-109, discusses the poem's development: "*Début* sous forme imprécative qui se termine par une apostrophe lyrique appelée par les Anciens *explosion pathétique*. *Définition*: l'ail est une sorte de poison qui, s'il est employé en cuisine, ne peut l'être que par des sorcières aux projets pernicieux. *Cause et effet*: 1) l'odeur qui met en fuite: a) l'ail ferait fuir des monstres furieux, b) l'odeur détourne d'elle [Creusa] Jason. 2) l'ail donne une sensation de brûlure, ce qu'Horace illustre par deux comparaisons: a) les vapeurs caniculaires, b) la tunique de Nessus." On lines 19-22, Colmant comments: "Nous passons le dernier effet ...." While much of his analysis is to the point, Colmant treats 19-22 as another effect, and fails to notice its relationship in form and content to 1-4 rather than to 5-18. That 5-8 constitute a "définition habilement développée" is not supported by any citation; on the contrary, the syntax is three simple questions. To take 9-14 as a development of the odor of garlic is without foundation. An odor theme is neither stated nor suggested. In the case of Creusa, the sensation is clearly burning; in the case of the bull, it is the same save that garlic is here an antidote to the animal's fire, the idea being that of fighting fire with fire. Colmant, in assuming that Medea's flight is from odor, has again missed a structural technique: the flight concludes the Jason-Medea episode just as her falling in love introduced it. Both items are narrative and irrelevant to the effect of garlic. There is, however, nothing to preclude the girl's reluctance as arising from the garlic on Maecenas' breath — here the penalty fits the crime. Porphyrion (on 21) is to the point: Id est: refutet puella savium tuum pro allii foetore, et in sponda lecta fugiat olentem virum.

[100] *Op. cit.* (above, n.IV.11), 68.

from real life, while the gift to Heracles is drawn from myth. The
pattern is: real life + real life; myth + myth; real life + myth.
Further relationships among the elements which are not immediately apparent:

	Agent	Administrator	Method	Purpose
1)	blood			
2)		witch		to kill
3)		witch		to win love
4)		witch	gift of clothing	to kill
5)				
6)	blood		gift of clothing	to win love

Noteworthy is the tragic reversal of 4) in 6). Medea knowingly
poisoned the gifts for Creusa to remove her rival. Deianira gave
the poisoned gift to Heracles to free him, she thought, of affection
for her rival; instead, it killed him. The choice of Horace to include 3), where the ointment on Jason protects rather than injures
him, is an unsolved problem. Giarratano[101] agrees with Castiglioni
that the oddity of a salutory drug amid the other five oppressive
elements merely reflects Horace's wish to select an item which
indicates "semplicemente la misteriosa miscela della maga" and
we might add the image of fire. It further seems possible that
Horace has to a degree become the victim of his central panel, the
Medea myth. He stresses the meeting and the parting and incidents
close in story time to each. Even as Creusa's murder shortly
precedes Medea's flight, so too must there be an incident early
after their falling in love, but the myth admits nothing noxious to
Jason at that point. The yoked bulls are perhaps our scapegoats.
    The only difficulty in linking epodes 2 and 3 is the assertion that
despite their common theme, country life, their tones vary: epode 3
is playful whereas epode 2 is invective. One is tempted to accept
epode 2 as invective and to link it with 4, 5, 6, 8, 10, 12 and 17.
The addition of epode 2 lends a pleasing symmetry to the arrangement of the male-female invective poems:

[101]   Op. cit. (above, n.III.6), 40.

2	4	5	6	8	10	12	17
M	M	F	M	F	M	F	F

Tempting as this scheme is, it must be rejected.

The question of the tone of epode 2 has evoked much discussion. How one is to reconcile the tone of apparent sincerity in the praise of country life (1-66) with the startling conclusion (67-70):

> haec ubi locutus faenerator Alfius,
>   iam iam futurus rusticus
> omnem redegit Idibus pecuniam,
>   quaerit Kalendis ponere.

has exercised the ingenuity of too many scholars. Boissier[102] believed that Horace was mocking his readers and that the joke was rendered even more cruel because the reader does not realize it until the end — he is duped to the very last verse.[103] Horace's reason Boissier explains:

Il était impatient de voir tant de gens admirer à froid la campagne; il voulait rire aux dépens de ceux qui, n'ayant aucune opinion personnelle, croient devoir prendre tous les goûts de la mode, en les exagérant.

The weakness of Boissier's argument is that he equates the failure of Alfius to pursue his ideal with not having "aucune opinion personnelle" and desiring to maintain currently fashionable tastes. The poem offers no evidence for this equation; nor does Boissier.

Another ingenious, if unconvincing, solution is that of Salanitro. He argues that the conclusion does not impart a tone to the epode, but rather indicates its effects. Horace himself has spoken the first sixty-six lines, and the last four should be read: *Haec ubi locutus* (*sum* = I, Horace), (he) *fenerator Alfius, iam iam futurus rusticus, omnem redegit Idibus pecuniam, quaerit Kalendis ponere* (*in praedio emendo*). Salanitro paraphrases:

L'usuraio Alfio, spinto dalle mie parole, si dispone a diventare proprie-

---

[102] G. Boissier, *Nouvelles promenades archéologiques* (Paris, 1886), 18-19. This position was recently reaffirmed by J. O'Brien, "Horace, Champion of the Country", *CB* 37 (1961), 33-35.
[103] The epode's second major division (67-70) contains the humorous and surprising conclusion: speaker, matter and tone have changed. Note, however, that the surprise is not as unprepared for as some may think. *Faenerator* (67) clearly recalls the *faenore* (4), and *omni* (4) is faintly recalled by *omnem* (69). The epode's last four lines play upon the hint in its first four lines.

tario di terreni. Infatti ha ritirato alle Idi tutto il denaro per investirlo
il di delle Calende diligentemente nella compra di campi.[104]

Against the opinions of Boissier and Salanitro as well as those
who find "bitter irony",[105] the hypocritical harangue of a money-
lender,[106] or "un quadro tutto roseo",[107] should be set the sane and
balanced judgments of Sellar, Campbell, Wilkinson and Fraenkel.
All four insist that the proportion of lines cannot be discounted
and that the humorously satiric conclusion is again another example of the Horatian tendency to check himself with a bit of commonplace irony when he is indeed at his most serious. The wisdom
of this interpretation is that it avoids the necessity of imagining
a particular setting and attitude on the part of Alfius and Horace
which the epode does not supply. Sellar, Campbell, Wilkinson and

---

[104]   Nino Salanitro, *L'epodo secondo di Orazio* (Catania, 1935), 13.
[105]   Plüss (above, n.IV.19) 133, who would explain much in the Epodes as
"sarcastic irony", favors the interpretation of an ungenuine desire for country
life. Orelli-Baiter-Hirschfelder comment (above, n.I.1) : "[Horace] inducit
Alfium, feneratorem ditissimum ... optima fide praedicantem innumerabilia
vitae rusticae gaudia ac delicias ... nulla inest εἰρωνεία. Verum εἰρωνεία
quattuor demum ultimis versiculis festive admodum et παρὰ προσδοκίαν pro-
rumpit nosque docet in eo uno elaborasse Horatium, ut hominem vel etiam
tunc viventem vel ex recentis satis notum ridiculum redderet. Etenim, cum iam
iam in eo esset, ut tot tantasque voluptates facili opera sibi pararet, velut invitus,
sed necessitudine quadam indolis suae coactus, ilico ad pristinam lucri cupidi-
tatem redit fenerator.
[106]   G. Curcio, "La tesi dell'Epodo 2 di Q. Orazio Flacco", *Miscellanea di
studi critici in onore di Ettore Stampini* (Torino, 1921), 29-34, concludes: "Alfio
avra divulgato una volta, servendosene come giustificazione a sollecitare i
debitori e liquidare i suoi crediti, che si sarebbe ritirato in campagna, ma in
realtà poi rimase in città." Wickham (above, n.III.6), 356, aptly notes: "... but
the character of the irony is due to the nature of the poem, it turns an Idyll into
an Epode. Its point is rather the strength of the 'ruling passion' ... than ... the
elaborate hypocrisy of a money-lender."
[107]   Giarratano (above, n.III.6), 28: "Non e serio [l'elogio campestre], perche
con altro tono e con altro metro Orazio avrebbe cantato le lodi della campagna,
se avesse espresso i suoi sentimenti, non quelli de Alfio. Questi non conosce
la vita dei campi, ma quando di tanto in tanto lo prende il tedio dei banchetti
fastosi, degli amori con le etere e specialmente della operazioni finanziarie che
lo tengono in ansia continua, se la figura come un quadro tutto roseo." Similarly,
Kiessling-Heinze (above, n.III.6), 491: "Der aufmerksame Leser bemerkt
auch wohl die gewollte Einseitigkeit des Gemäldes, das ohne im eizelnen zu
karikieren, die Mühen und Sorgen der Landwirtschaft kaum andeutet und
alles ins rosigste Licht des Vergnügens und Behagens taucht."

Fraenkel are correctly guided by the normal technique of Horace where immediate evidence is incomplete.[108]

Epodes 11, 13, 14 and 15 comprise a last group of poems devoted to a major theme: Erotic and Sympotic.[109] 11 and 14 have an especially close relationship. Both epodes are addressed to friends of Horace; 11 to Pettius (about whom nothing is known[110]), and 14 to Maecenas. To the former Horace complains that he finds no delight in writing poetry now that he has been stricken by an *amore gravi* (11.1-2); to the latter Horace complains about being urged to complete his book of epodes when (14.6-8):

> deus deus nam me vetat
> inceptos olim, promissum carmen, iambos
> ad umbilicum adducere.[111]

[108] The locus classicus for the interpretation of the tone of this epode is still W. Y. Sellar, *The Roman Poets of the Augustan Age. Horace and the Elegiac Poets*[2] (Oxford, 1899), 130, parts of which Fraenkel (above, n.IV.11), 61, quotes with additional arguments of his own. See also Campbell (above, n.IV. 21), 140-141, and L. P. Wilkinson, *Horace and His Lyric Poetry* (Cambridge, 1951), 55: "But as so often his irony lies in wait for his seriousness; and those who would tie him down to one or the other misunderstand his nature." E. H. Haight, "A note on Horace's Second Epode", *CW* 4 (1918), 44-45, refers to *Ars Poetica* 14-17 as evidence that in epode 2 Horace attempts to avoid the danger of the "purple patch". "He will write no passage about nature that seems too highly colored. His most brilliant description he will set in iambic lines as more of a satire than an idyl ... to remove any danger of a charge of false emotionalism in his tone." Steele Commager, *The Odes of Horace. A Critical Study* (New Haven, 1962), 107: "Yet the essence of the poem lies in the fact that Horace shows himself neither exclusively a sentimentalist nor exclusively a cynic. He is simply aware that two attitudes exist — and may collide."

[109] Despite W. Wili's insistence on the principle of *variatio*, he remarks in a section entitled "Lyrisches Vorspiel" (above, n.IV,15), 60-61: "In der kleinen Iambensammlung heben sich vier Gedichte auffällig, die Epoden 11, 13, 14 und 15. Im Negativen ist das Gemeinsame, dass sie alle des persönlich Iambischen, sowie des Politischen entbehren, aber auch des hässlichen Wortes. Ihnen ist weiter eigentümlich, dass sie alle und als einzige dieser Gedichte von ihrer freundlichen und bestimmten Neigung zu Liebe und Wein erzählen. Sie erfüllen also den Sinn des Iambus, der höhnen und spotten will, in keiner Weise." G. Pasquali, *Orazio lirico* (Firenze, 1920), 719, likewise links 11, 13, 14 and 15: "E in quegli epodi spuntano per la prima volta motivi e immagini che ricompariranno nelle odi. ..."

[110] Porphyrion (on 11.1) simply calls Pettius a *contubernalis*, a relationship which can be gathered from the poem itself. Compare Porphyrion on 12.23, 13.1, and *Odes* 1.6.1.

[111] The *deus*, of course, is Cupid.

In both epodes, a *gravis amor* prevents Horace from writing poetry.

It has been the practice of Horatian criticism to take note of the fifteenth epode as one of a group of poems which are elegiac and Hellenistic in tone, and focus on the theme of love. Although richly praised for its beauty, the piece has not received the individual analysis so artful a composition deserves. The purpose then of this section is to attempt to interpret and relate the poem's structure and meaning.

Epode 15 admits a bipartite division (1-16 and 17-24). In I, Horace addresses Neaera; in II, he apostrophizes his unnamed rival.[112] This division is so sharp and clear-cut that, although II is carefully prepared for in I, the epode could nonetheless have ended at line 16 with the reader entirely satisfied with its structural completeness.

I is built around the related concepts of oath and resolution; the first is almost forsworn[113] and the second is weakly conditional. Neaera's formal lover's oath comprises lines 1-10, the first six lines describing the occasion of the swearing of the oath and the last four lines reporting its contents. Horace begins the occasion of the oath with a couplet painting nature's setting richly adorned with romantic details: night, clear sky and moon shining amid the lesser stars (1-2). We might next have expected a close-up of Neaera tightly embracing Horace and then, only after the setting and the lovers had been portrayed, to be told that she took an oath, this last to be followed by the details of the oath. But Horace has upset this obvious pattern by intruding the swearing of the oath between the descriptions of the setting and the principals in order to allow the hammer blow (3):

cum tu magnorum numen laesura deorum

[112]   Giarratano, *op. cit.*, (above, n.III.6) 99: "L'epodo si divide in due parti, perchè il poeta prima si rivolge a Neera (1-16), poi al fortunato rivale (17-24)." Plüss, *op. cit.* (above, n.IV.19) 96, structures: A 1-10; B I 11-16, II 17-23; C 24. This very curious division is based on his peculiar interpretation of the "bitter irony" of the book. The weakness of Plüss' method was nicely pointed out by one of his reviewers, R. Cahen, *Bulletin Critique* 5 (1905), 91-97.
[113]   Porphyrion on 3: ad eventum refert, quasi cum iuraret iam perfidiam fallendi in animo haberet.

to fall earlier and more effectively between the tenderness of night and the tight embrace of her pliant arms. Aside from the artful placement of the future active participle *laesura*, [114] in this line of six words each contains one "u", "m" occurs five times, "n" three times and the first four feet of the hexameter are spondees. The net result of the spondaic heaviness and assonance is gravity. What makes the participle in this context even more effective is the sequence of tenses: *erat ... fulgebat ... laesura ... iurabas*, which causes the future to clash violently with the imperfect tenses which encompass it.

Lines 7-10 comprise her oath as recalled in indirect discourse: three (an accumulation Horace is partial to) *dum* clauses and the future infinitive *fore*. So long as three ἀδύνατα do not take place, their love will be reciprocal. The structural significance of the details of the *dum* clauses as they relate to II (17-24) will be considered shortly; for the present it should be noted that I accept Housman's zeugma in line 7.[115]

The structure of Horace's resolution (11-16) is quite straightforward. He tells Neaera that if he has any manliness she will suffer; and despite the syntax of 12 which makes it dependent upon 13-14, its ties to line 11 are closer as they both develop the

---

[114] Campbell, *op. cit.* (above, n.IV.21), 142: "The first half-dozen lines of this piece are one of the very few passages of real poetry in the whole of the book; in the third line the future participle is especially good; though neither one of them knew she was to be false, it was already destined."

[115] A. E. Housman, "Elucidations of Latin Poets", *CR* 15 (1901), 404-406: "... the meaning of Horace's words is the following: '*dum lupus pecori infestus* (*terreret ovilia*, or what you will,) *et Orion nautis infestus turbaret hibernum mare.*'" Giarratano, *op. cit.* (above, n.III.6), 100, and Fraenkel, *op. cit.* (above, n.IV.11), 67 note 6, agree. Other interpretations with or without emendations have been offered. I note, besides the standard *foret*, four of these in chronological order. M. Graf, "Die 15. Epode des Horaz", *Xenien* (München, 1891) 13-19, emended *pecori lupus* to *fureret notus*. S. Allen, "On Horace, Epode XV., 1-10; and on Virgil, *Aeneid* IX., 339", *CR* 16 (1902), 305-306, thinks *pecori lupus* a corruption of *pecoralibus*, "cattle pens". E. H. Alton, "The Zeugma in Horace's Epode XV", *CR* 19 (1905) 215-216, suggested the emendation *lips*: "*Lips* might easily have been mistaken for an abbreviation of *lupus* (*lupš*)." J. P. Postgate, "On Horace Epode XV.5 and Seneca *Herc. Oet.* 335 sqq.", *CR* 19 (1905), 217-218, reads: "*dum lupus infestus pecori turbaret* (neuter, sc. '*per ovilia*' or '*in ovilibus*') *et Orion nautis infestus hibernum mare turbaret* (active)."

idea of *virtus* and *vir*, and together with these terms perhaps play on the word Flaccus.[116] 11-12 are the key couplet of Horace's conditional resolution, with 13-14 and 15-16 spelling out clearly the particulars. Horace will not brook a rival, but will himself seek an equal, presumably a girl who can be faithful even as he has been to Neaera (13-14). Nor is Neaera to hope that her beauty will compel Horace's submission to her ways,[117] for his *virtus* is concretized as *constantia* unyielding,[118] especially if backed by a deep-seated grief (15-16). Despite this bravado, the two *si* clauses (12 and 16) make it abundantly clear that Horace's resolution is even less reliable than Neaera's oath. His sham resolution is in fact merely a thinly veiled plea for Neaera to mend her morals. The careful symmetry of 11-16 may be appreciated at a glance:

```
o dolitura (first words) ─────────┐  11
  ┌─nam si                         │  12
  │ ┌─non                          │  13
  │ │ et                           │  14
  │ └─nec                          │  15
  └─si          dolor (last word) ─┘  16
```

The deliberate pattern of alliteration again is striking:

```
      A    1    1      2       3
   o dolitura mea multum virtute Neaera        11
     3    4     5  6      2
   nam si quid in Flacco viri est,             12
```

[116] Giarratano, *op. cit.* (above, n.III.6), 101: "Spesso il nome proprio usato invece del pronome denota il pathos. ..." So Kiessling-Heinze, *op. cit.* (above, n.III.6), 544, who state flatly: "... ein Spiel mit der ursprünglichen Bedeutung von *flaccus* 'schlaff' scheint mir dem Ethos der Stelle nicht angemessen. ..." The contrary is suggested as possible by Cruquius on 12: fortasse per anthypophoram obiecti convicii alludit ad adiectivum flaccus; quasi Horat. flaccidis et demissis auribus, in re Venerea illi non satisfecisset. V. Ussani, *Le liriche di Orazio*[2] (Torino, 1922) 1.41, is more imaginative: "Par quasi de cogliere in questo verso un'eco di corrucci antecedenti, nei quali egli la minacciava della *virtus* ed ella rispondeva mottegiando il *cognomen* dell'amante: 'La tua *virtus*? Oh! tu non sei un *vir*, sei un *flaccus* (un imbelle).'"

[117] Scholia χ I: Diceret illa; pulchra sum nimis et ideo quicquid faciam, mihi subiacebis precando.

[118] I follow the MSS reading *offensae* (15) against Bentley's conjecture *offensi*. For a spirited and sensitive refutation of *offensi* see Olivier, *op. cit.* (above, n.IV.20), 121-124.

3   6   7   3
non feret adsiduas *potiori* te dare *noctes,*   13

                5   7
et quaeret *iratus* *parem,*   14

3   4   6   8   8   6
nec semel offensae cedet constantia formae,   15

  4 8   5   A
si *certus intrarit dolor*   16

II (17-24) abruptly (*et tu*) turns from Neaera to Horace's rival. The unit is built on contrast and reversal, of which *felicior* is the first note in the picture of the man's good fortune that fills six lines (17-22). In 17-18 the rival struts proud over Horace's misfortune and in 19-22 he is conceded (*licebit*) that which Horace lacks: wealth (in the forms of cattle, land and gold), invulnerability to death and handsomeness. We here again have an example of Horace's affinity for grouping by threes: three things are granted,[119] the first of which, wealth, is not stated as such but is itself represented by three items. But in 23-24, Horace will have the last (if bitter) laugh. The whole presents a tidy architectural study in balance and chiasmus:

	Key Words		Total Lines	Lines
es felicior	et tu nunc	17		2
(meo) malo (last word)		18		
sis		19		
tibique Pactolus fluat (first words)		20		4
nec te Pythagorae fallant (first words)		21		
vincas		22		
maerebis		23		2
ego risero (last word)	ast ego vicissim	24		

We may now take note of the epode's linear allocation:

$$24 = 16 (= 10 [=6+4] + 6) + 8 (= 2 + 4 + 2)$$

The second primary unit of eight lines is one half the sixteen line total of the first primary unit. The first and second primary units achieve further symmetry by composition of subordinate units. The

---

[119]   Comm. Cruq. on 22: Tria commemorat, quibus amor nascitur et augetur, nimirum, divitias, sapientiam, et pulchritudinem. Idem facit Virg. in 2. Ecloga.

central panel of each comprises four lines in which a catalogue of three items is contained. Each panel is preceded and followed by an equal number of lines (6 and 2, respectively).

In confronting some of the more subtle but not less real relationships of I to II, let us first of all recall several items in the catalogue of Neaera's oath (7-10) and several included in the catalogue of the good fortune of Horace's rival (17-22):

pecus (7)	pecus (19)
nautis infestus Orion (7)	Pythagorae renati (21)
turbaret mare (8)	Pactolus fluat (20)
Apollo (9)	Nireus (22)

That *pecori* (7) and *pecore* (19) are repetitious, and that the sea in turmoil and the flowing Pactolus are two instances of liquid imagery (sea and river) might be dismissed as examples of the many coincidences likely to appear in poetry. One could further note by way of curiosity that while the hostility between wolf and cattle and the turbulence of the sea are to guarantee Nearea's fidelity, strangely enough the young man with whom she betrays this fidelity is rich in cattle and far from being on a troubled sea he has the Pactolus flowing with gold for himself and presumably for his beloved. His wealth and success over Horace recall the poet's complaint on another occasion when he had lost out in the game of love (11.11-12):

'contrane lucrum nil valere candidum / pauperis ingenium?'

Were this all, the curiosity might be noted and dismissed. But it is not.

Let us turn to a portion of another poem of Horace (*Odes* 1.28.9-22):

> ... habentque
> Tartara Panthoiden iterum Orco
> demissum, quamvis clipeo Troiana refixo
> tempora testatus nihil ultra
> nervos atque cutem morti concesserat atrae,
> iudice te non sordidus auctor
> naturae verique. sed omnis una manet nox
> et calcanda semel via leti.
> dant alios Furiae torvo spectacula Marti;
> exitio est avidum mare nautis;

mixta senum ac iuvenum densentur funera; nullum
   saeva caput Proserpina fugit.
me quoque devexi rapidus comes Orionis[120]
   Illyricis Notus obruit undis.

This passage is appropriate for two reasons. First, it makes clear,
without going beyond the text of Horace, that line 21:

   nec te Pythagorae fallant arcana renati

does not simply mean that he knows the mysteries of philosophy
but that he knows the secret of the conquest of death. Pythagoras
argued for the death of flesh and sinew, but as for the *anima*, it took
its abode in another body. In the ode, Horace refers to the claim
of Pythagoras that he was the reincarnation of Euphorbus, a Trojan
hero slain by Menelaos.[121] To substantiate his claim, Pythagoras
selected a shield, hanging in the temple of Argos, which was shown
to be that of Euphorbus. On *iterum* (10) Pseudo-Acron explains:
Quia saepe mortuus est transeunte anima eius in alios. Second, the
passage shows clearly for us the relation by contrast of the *nauta*
doomed to die and Pythagoras (or Horace's rival who knows the
philosopher's *arcana*) who is immune to death. The ode also
associates with the sailor both Orion and the sea as instruments of
his destruction even as the epode does.
   That line 22:

   formaque vincas Nirea

harkens back to line 9:

   intonsosque agitaret Apollinis aura capillos

is not at once apparent. The relationship is not intended to be a
matter of one-for-one equation. Handsome Apollo's hair streaming
in the breeze is appropriate enough as a component of a lover's
oath, but warned as we were by (3):

   cum tu magnorum numen laesura deorum

it quietly hints at "the other man". And when this other man appears he is favorably compared with handsome Nireus. The

---

[120] Pseudo-Acron: Ortus enim occasus Orionis tempestuosi sunt; ideo et
comitem eius notum ventum dixit.
[121] *Iliad* 17.69.

positive link between Apollo and Nireus is furnished by Horace in *Odes* 3.20.13-16 where the picture of Nearchus, Nireus and Ganymede is that of Apollo in our epode:

> fertur et leni recreare vento
> sparsum odoratis umerum capillis,
> qualis aut Nireus fuit aut aquosa
> raptus ab Ida.

But the comparison of Horace's rival with Nireus is not wholly flattering. Nireus is listed among the heroes in the catalogue of *Iliad* 2, and Homer, to be sure, tells us that Nireus was the most handsome of the Greeks (Achilles excepted) who waged war at Troy. At the same time Homer describes him as a weakling and on that account followed but by few men (2.671-675):

> Νιρεὺς αὖ Σύμηθεν ἄγε τρεῖς νῆας ἐΐσας,
> Νιρεὺς 'Αγλαΐης υἱὸς Χαρόποιό τ' ἄνακτος,
> Νιρεύς, ὃς κάλλιστος ἀνὴρ ὑπὸ Ἴλιον ἦλθε
> τῶν ἄλλων Δαναῶν μετ' ἀμύμονα Πηλεΐωνα·
> ἀλλ' ἀλαπαδνὸς ἔην, παῦρος δέ οἱ εἵπετο λαός.

Nireus' deficiency of Homeric *aretê* recalls the Roman *virtus* (twice noted in *virtute* and *viri* and specified as *constantia*) of the ousted Horace.[122]

Like Catullus in 8, Horace in epode 15 attempts to steel himself against his unfaithful lady's charms. But he struggles with doubtful success. Horace's prophecy to Neaera's new favorite (23):

> heu heu translatos alio maerebis amores

sounds more like a feeble attempt to frighten him away than a threat; its relevance to Horace's present condition and the poem's essence is:

> heu heu translatos tibi dulcis maereo amores.

Of the setting of epode 13 we know nothing beyond the fact that a *horrida tempestas* has arisen whereupon Horace exhorts his friends

---

[122] Demetrius, *de elocutione* 61-62, notes the devices of anaphora and disjunction in 2.671-674 that magnify the mean Nireus and his meagre following of three ships to the point of making him a character as easily remembered as Achilles and Odysseus.

to dispel their cares with wine and song, even as Chiron once advised Achilles. The conviviality of friends anointed with Persian nard and joining in the pleasures of drink and song serves here to make them forgetful of life's anxieties and to have conversation take a different turn: *cetera mitte loqui*. The scene recalls by way of contrast the pathetic banquets of epode 11 at which Horace, overcome by love, could only exhibit a telltale *languor et silentium* and finally when flushed with *fervidiore mero* spewed forth the bitterness in his heart. In 13 we meet the mellowed Horace of the *Odes*.

We have already discussed the thematic classification of epode 13 and rejected the inclusion of it under the heading of political or national, simply because of the lack of direct supporting evidence either internal or from the book as a whole. The position which views the epode as a war poem rests on the Horatian usage of a storm as a symbol for civil strife and the choice of the paradigm drawn from the occasion of the Trojan War.[123] Both points are not without weight. To be sure, stormy weather is proverbial for war, and the advice of Chiron to Achilles evokes a war setting. On the other hand, the storm symbol is foreign to the book of *Epodes* and those who would so interpret the poem rely on the *Odes*; but here chronology must act as a brake, for one is free to so theorize only in the light of the first three books of *Odes* which are some seven years away from publication. Are we really prepared to say that the genial advice of epode 13, as it appears in the book of *Epodes* in the year 30 B.C., suggests in the close association with epodes 11, 14 and 15 predominantly the tense conflict atmosphere of epodes 1, 7, 9 and 16 where the poet tells us expressly that his subject is war? Even if we imagine that the poem reflects the atmosphere of the defeated republican forces at Philippi

---

[123] See especially Campbell, *op. cit.* (above, n.IV.21), 143, and Commager, *op. cit.* (above, n.IV.108), 172-173, though he does say that the epode is not strictly political: "The myth's ultimate implications force the poem to a new context, and we realize that Horace's advice to his friends is of the same seriousness as Chiron's to Achilles. *Rapiamus, amici, occasionem de die* (3-4) does not refer to a single day any more than does *carpe diem*. Horace writes to his friends about youth and age, modified forms of life and death, just as all men are embarked upon a modified form of Achilles' journey."

or of the vanquished faction on some other occasion, the absence
of direct references must at least lead us to conclude that Horace
was content to let the poem speak or remain silent for itself and
that if the poem did date from the period of Philippi the poet was
also content to pass over gracefully his unhappy role in the opposition to Octavian. My position remains one of insistence that
Horace is capable of saying what he wants to say and of making
his meaning clear beyond doubt. What is clear and beyond doubt
in epode 13 and therefore what Horace's audience of 30 B.C. must
have gotten first and foremost from the poem is that wine, song,
congenial companionship and perhaps benign change ushered in
by some god or divine power are the answer to life's anxious cares,
whatever their kind may be.

We may now safely group the *Epode* on the basis of the four
major themes:

>   Political or National: 1, 7, 9, 16
>   Country Life: 2, 3
>   Invective: 4, 5, 6, 8, 10, 12, 17
>   Erotic and Sympotic: 11, 13, 14, 15

The first half of the book (1-8) opens with an epode (1) of the
political or national; two epodes (2, 3) of country life follow, and
a group of four epodes (4, 5, 6, 8) of invective (the series broken only
by an epode [7] of the political or national) closes the first half of
the book. The second half of the book (9-17) opens with an epode
(9) of the political or national and an epode (10) of invective and
closes with an epode (16) of the political or national and an epode
(17) of invective. Centered within the second half is a group of
four epodes (11, 13, 14, 15) of the erotic and sympotic (the series
broken only by an epode [12] of invective).

Notice has already been taken of the position of the two Actium
epodes (1 and 9), each at the beginning of a half of the book. The
companion pieces 7 and 16, completing the group of political or
national epodes, stand each as the next to the last poem of a half
of the book. Further notes of symmetry are also evident. Each
half ends with an epode of invective (8 and 17); in both cases a
woman is attacked. In both halves in the first invective poem
encountered (4 and 10) a man is attacked. The dominant theme of

the first half is invective (four epodes of invective, two of political
or national, two of country life); the dominant theme of the second
half is the erotic and sympotic (four epodes of the erotic and sympotic, three of invective, two of the political or national). The
disposition of the dominant thematic clusters of each half is
chiastic relation to one another:

4	5	6	7	8	11	12	13	14	15
C	C	C		C	D		D	D	D

The themes of 7 and 12 are different; it should also be noted that
the dominant thematic clusters are not arranged with regard to
numerical symmetry to each other.

The dominant theme of the *Epodes* as an entire book is invective.
The dominant theme of the first half is secured both by the number
of invective poems and the clustering of them; in the second half the
dominant theme is the erotic and sympotic secured again by the
number of poems and the clustering of them. But invective runs
a close second in this half of the book with three epodes of this
type (10, 12, 17). Notice how the erotic and sympotic cluster is
interrupted by 12 — a particularly vicious poem — and that 17
ends the book. Despite the fact that the erotic and sympotic is
dominant in the second half, yet the number and disposition of
the invective poems will not allow us to forget that the dominant
theme of the book as a whole is invective. The *Epodes* remain
essentially *iambi*.

Arrangement of the Epodes by Major Themes and Dominant
Thematic Clusters.

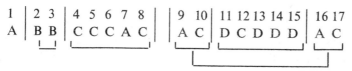

1	2 3	4 5 6 7 8	9 10	11 12 13 14 15	16 17
A	B B	C C C A C	A C	D C D D D	A C

A = Political or National
B = Country Life
C = Invective
D = Erotic and Sympotic

V

SOME ASPECTS OF BALANCE IN THE FIRST AND SECOND HALVES OF THE BOOK OF *EPODES*

Notice has already been taken of the arrangement of the eight companion pieces and the balanced effect it lends both halves of the book of *Epodes*. Four of the companion pieces appear in the first half and four in the second half. 5, 7 and 8 are arranged chiastically with 12, 16 and 17 around the pivot point, epode 9, which is itself in balance with epode 1. Poems 6 and 14 (both of which occupy the sixth position in their respective halves), though different in spirit and major theme, have a strong affinity. In 6 the poet announces his mission. Like a faithful shepherd-dog or a bull with sharp horns Horace stands ready to counterattack with his *iambi* the aggressor, the cowardly defamer. In 14, a *quasi recusatio*, we find the poet, stricken by love, unable to complete his mission. He complains about Maecenas' continued pressure for the completion of the *Epodes* and alleges that love prevents him from *iambos ad umbilicum adducere*. Another note of balance is achieved by the addressing of a second poem in each half to Maecenas, one playful (3) and one serious (14).

The careful arrangement of *Odes* 1.1-3 so that each poem addresses itself to a different one of the three most important men in Horace's adult life from the time when Vergil first introduced him to Maecenas has rightly been noted time and again. Ode 1 dedicates the first three books of *Odes* to Maecenas. Ode 2 suggests that Augustus may in fact be Mercury incarnate, descended upon earth to save the Roman state. Ode 3 is a *propempticon* for Vergil. There is a strong probability that the arrangement of these three owes more than a little to the prior arrangement of the initial poems of the first and second halves of the *Epodes*.[1] Both epodes 1 and 9 are addressed to Maecenas and stress the friendship between Maecenas and Horace, and again in both poems (especially 9) the fate of Octavian at Actium figures strongly. In the *Odes*, Maecenas and Octavian are each given a separate ode. What then of the position of ode 3, a *propempticon* for Vergil? Horace wrote two poems of this genre. Epode 10 was the first of the two to be written. In Fraenkel's masterful treatment of epode 10, he rightly argues that the epode seems to owe its existence to Horace's desire to produce a similar (not an imitation) venomous *propempticon* after the fashion of one which appeared in the *Epodes* of Archilochus. As such, an appropriate target of attack had to be selected by Horace and he chose the poet Mevius. Epode 10 singles out Mevius as its target for no other reason than that he has body odor, a fault which receives a mere passing reference (*olentem*) and is not further treated. Clearly, the reason for the selection lies beyond what the epode states or suggests. Mevius was a suitable target because he was a literary enemy of the poet's friend Vergil. Vergil testifies to the bitter antipathy:

Qui Bavium non odit, amet tua carmina, Maevi, / atque idem iungat vulpes et mulgeat hircos.[2]

Epode 10 and ode 1.3 are then related by genre, by position, and by the poets involved. Ode 1.3 is a direct tribute to Vergil (*animae dimidium meae*); epode 10 as an attack on Vergil's poet enemy is an indirect tribute.

We must now consider the significance of epode 2. Epode 2, some scholars have claimed, takes its cue from the *Georgics* of Vergil and linguistic parallels to this effect have been cited as proof.[3] That linguistic parallels are conscious borrowings or intended references to another work is on the whole difficult to

---

[1] T. Frank, "Vergil's Apprenticeship", *CP* 15 (1920), 23-38, has already noticed that the position of epode 2 as the second in the collection suggests, on the basis of *Odes* 1.1-3, that Horace intended to compliment Vergil. Frank, however, says nothing of the significance of the positions of epodes 9 and 10, and their relationship to epodes 1 and 2 as well as *Odes* 1.1-3.
[2] *Eclogues* 3.90-91. Cf. Servius on *Georgics* 1.210, and Porphyrion on *Epodes* 10.1.
[3] Compare *Georgics* 2.493 ff.

prove and when one has, as in the case of the *Georgics*, over 2,000 lines to scrutinize for parallels this argument becomes even less convincing.[4] We must therefore frankly admit that this line of argument is by itself inconclusive. Several other factors, however, must be kept in mind. As Duckworth[5] has already clearly demonstrated, the influence of the two poets upon each other is evident in a multitude of instances. They read, discussed and were influenced by each other's works. Probability therefore is against coincidence and in favor of a relationship between the epode and the *Georgics*. One need only cite the problem of the relationship of eclogue 4 and epode 16.

From a biographic point of view chances are good that epode 2 arises in connection with the gift of the Sabine farm to Horace, a later result of Vergil's introduction of Horace to Maecenas. Epode 2, we should remember, follows immediately upon Horace's assertion in epode 1: *satis superque me benignitas tua ditavit*, which must refer to the Sabine farm.[6] The juxtaposition of the two poems meant to be read the one after the other cannot be ignored. Finally, both the *Georgics* and epode 2, as contemporaneous *laudationes* of country life in keeping with the Augustan program of reform, are not likely to have been written in isolation from one another. It is then very probable (we cannot say certain) that the second epode, like the tenth, contains an indirect tribute to Vergil.[7]

---

[4] T. Frank, *op. cit.* (above, n.V.1), 23-33, argues that epode 2 imitates the *Culex* by way of complimenting Vergil and subsequently Vergil returned the compliment by imitating epode 2 in the second book of the *Georgics*. This position was restated in Frank's *Vergil. A Biography* (New York, 1922), 142-143, and more recently held as "not improbable" by H. Wagenvoort, *Studies in Roman Literature, Culture and Religion* (Leiden, 1956), 79-83. This contention rests on two points difficult to prove: (1) that the *Culex* is by Vergil, and (2) that epode 2 was one of the earliest composed epodes. It seems far safer and simpler to take epode 2 as a compliment to the *Georgics*.

[5] Above, n.IV.71.

[6] So Porphyrion on 1.31: Donatum sibi in Sabinis fundum a Maecenate Horatius saepe testatus est.

[7] Perhaps too *Epodes* 3.4 (*o dura messorum ilia!*) playfully recalls *Eclogues* 2.10-11 where Thestylis prepares a *moretum* for the reapers.

THE INFLUENCE OF THE METRICAL ORDER
OF THE ARCHILOCHIAN *EPODES*

In his attempt to reconstruct the *Epodes* of Archilochus, François Lasserre took as a starting point the evidence of the metricians Servius, Hephaestion and Marius Plotius. His method was to note carefully the order in which the metricians cited Archilochian metres for the reason that:

On sait que les métriciens ont l'habitude, lorsqu'ils citent un exemple, de le choisir au début du poème susceptible de le leur fournir et, naturellement, dans le premier poème qui se presente à eux de la série qui les intéresse. Cette façon de procéder s'explique aisément par le fait que les textes qu'ils étudient étaient édités sur des rouleaux de papyrus et qu'ils ne pouvaient en prendre connaissance et relever ce qu'ils y cherchaient qu'à mesure qu'ils les déroulaient.[1]

By correlating the order of metrical citations, Lasserre believed that he could uncover the metrical order of the *Epodes* of Archilochus. He further proposed that in his *Epodes* Horace was following the metrical order of the Archilochian book of *Epodes*. Lasserre also claimed that Horace in epodes 11-16 drew his inspiration not only from the metrics of Archilochus

... mais aussi de leur propos, avec une fidélité qui devient systématique à partir du moment où le plan de son livre se conforme rigoureusement à celui de son modèle, c'est-à-dire dans toute sa seconde partie.[2]

Lasserre's reconstruction of both the metrical order and the contents of the epodes to which Horace is said to have rigorously conformed cannot be judged a success. Lasserre's reviewers[3]

---

[1] François Lasserre, *Les Épodes d'Archiloque* (Paris, 1950), 19.
[2] *Ibid.*, 23.
[3] For reviews see: J. C. Kamerbeck, *Mnemosyne* 3 (1950), 345-347; R.

generally expressed admiration for the undertaking, criticism of his methods, cautious disbelief and attacked various assignments of Archilochian fragments to particular epodes. None, however, has examined the basic premise of Lasserre, namely, that when the metricians cite the metres of Archilochus they cite them in the order the metres appeared in the book of *Epodes*.[4] Let us first of all state flatly that Lasserre's basic premise rests on a failure to examine or understand the organizational principles at work in the treatises of the metricians.

Let us consider Lasserre's first metrician, Servius Honoratus. Lasserre notes that in chapter 9, *de diversis metrorum generibus*, of Servius' *de centum metris* the following Archilochian metres are cited in this order:

13   Archilochium constat paroemiaco et ithyphallico ...
(◡ – ᴗ – ᴗ – ◌ | – ◡ – ◡ – ◌)

18   Archilochium constat tetrametro bucolico et tribus trochaeis ...
(– ᴗ – ᴗ – ᴗ – ᴗ | – ◡ – ◡ – ◌)

20   Archilochium constat penthemimeri dactylica et dimetro iambico acatalecto ...
(– ᴗ – ᴗ – | ◡ – ◡ – ◡ – ᴗᴗ)

21   Archilochium constat dimetro iambico acatalecto et penthemimeri dactylica ...
(◡ – ◡ – ◡ – ◡ – | – ᴗ – ᴗᴗ)

Lasserre then concludes that these four metres appeared in this order in the poems of Archilochus.

Let us take a look at the organization of chapter 9 of Servius as well as the organization of the whole book. The *de centum metris*

Cantarella, *Aevum* 24 (1950), 507-509; J. Labarbe, *AC* 20 (1951), 174-180; A. Colonna, *Doxa* 4 (1951), 77-79; F. Della Corte, *GIF* 4 (1951), 163-167; G. Morelli, *Maia* 4 (1951) 150-154; P. Chantraine, *RPh* 26 (1952), 77-78; J. A. Davison, *CR* 2 (1952), 18-19; O. Masson, *Gnomon* 24 (1952), 310-316; A. Rivier, *REG* 65 (1952), 464-468; L. Castiglioni, *Prolegomena* 1 (1952), 132-137; R. Lattimore, *CP* 48 (1953), 40-41; F. Stoessel, *AJP* 74 (1953), 296-302; E. L. Highbarger, *CW* 46 (1953), 87-88; A. Lesky, *AAHG* 7 (1954), 9-11; Q. Cataudella, *Paideia* 11 (1956), 62-63.
[4] F. Adrados, "Nueva reconstrucción de los epodos de Arquíloco", *Emerita* 23 (1955), 1-78, points out arbitrary features within Lasserre's subsequent arrangements of metres, but his objections do not address the more basic consideration here raised.

contains one hundred metres divided into nine categories: *de iambicis, de trochaicis, de dactylicis, de anapaesticis, de choriambicis, de antispasticis, de ionicis a maiore, de ionicis a minore, de diversis.* Note the order of the chapters of metres with regard to the syllables of which the basic foot is composed:

(1) iamb: ∪ –
(2) trochee: – ∪ (the opposite of 1)
(3) dactyl: – ∪∪ (adds a short syllable to 2)
(4) anapest: ∪∪ – (the reverse of 3)
(5) choriamb: – ∪∪ – (prefaces a long syllable to 4)
(6) antipast: ∪ – – ∪ (the opposite of 5)
(7) ionic a maiore: – – ∪∪ (begins the ionic section)
(8) ionic a minore: ∪∪ – – (the opposite of 7)
(9) diversa: various

Again, note the fact that the chapters also proceed from the smallest number of syllables in the basic foot to the largest:

iamb and trochee: two syllables
dactyl and anapest: three syllables
choriamb, antispast and both ionics: four syllables

The organization of each of the first eight metrical sections is also based on the mathematical principle of smallest to largest; no effort is made to juxtapose or otherwise arrange the metres of any particular author:

DE IAMBICIS

Name	Composition
1. Aristophanium	monometrum hypercatalectum
2. Euripidium	dimetrum brachycatalectum
3. Anacreontium	dimetrum catalecticum
4. Archilochium	dimetrum acatalecticum
5. Alcaicum	dimetrum hypercatalectum
6. Alcmanium	trimetrum brachycatalectum
7. Hipponactium	trimetrum catalecticum
8. Archilochium	trimetrum acatalectum
9. Hipponactium	trimetrum acatalectum claudum
10. Anacreontium	trimetrum hypercatalectum
11. Aristophanium	tetrametrum brachycatalectum

12.	Aristophanium	tetrametrum catalecticum
13.	Anacreontium	tetrametrum acatalectum

DE TROCHAICIS

14.	Pancratium	monometrum hypercatalectum
15.	Ithyphallicum	dimetrum brachycatalectum
16.	Euripidium	dimetrum catalecticum
17.	Alcmanium	dimetrum acatalectum
18.	Bacchylidium	dimetrum hypercatalectum
19.	Sapphicum	trimetrum brachycatalectum
20.	Archilochium	trimetrum catalecticum
21.	Sotadicum	trimetrum acatalectum
22.	Sapphicum	trimetrum acatalectum
23.	Sotadicum	trimetrum hypercatalectum
24.	Archilochium	tetrametrum catalecticum
25.	Hipponactium	tetrametrum catalecticum claudum
26.	Anacreontium	tetrametrum acatalectum

DE DACTYLICIS

27.	Adonium	dimetrum catalecticum
28.	Hymenaicum	dimetrum acatalectum
29.	Archilochium	dimetrum hypercatalectum
30.	Alcmanium	trimetrum catalecticum
31.	Simonidium	trimetrum acatalectum
32.	Alcmanium	trimetrum hypercatalectum
33.	Archilochium	tetrametrum catalecticum
34.	Alcmanium	tetrametrum acatalectum
35.	Alcmanium	tetrametrum hypercatalectum
36.	Stesichorium	pentametrum catalecticum
37.	Simonidium	pentametrum acatalectum
38.	Choerilium	pentametrum hypercatalectum
39.	Heroicum	hexametrum catalecticum
40.	Bucolicum	hexametrum catalecticum
41.	Ibycium	hexametrum acatalectum
42.	Alcmanium	hexametrum hypercatalectum
43.	Stesichorium	heptametrum catalecticum
44.	Ibycium	heptametrum acatalectum

45. Ibycium   heptametrum hypercatalectum

DE ANAPAESTICIS

46. Threnicum   monometrum acatalectum
47. Choricum   monometrum hypercatalectum
48. Aristophanium   dimetrum brachycatalectum
49. Paroemiacum   dimetrum catalecticum
50. Pindaricum   dimetrum acatalectum
51. Alcmanium   dimetrum hypercatalectum
52. Archebulium   dimetrum acatalectum
53. Pindaricum   trimetrum brachycatalectum
54. Alcmanium   trimetrum catalecticum
55. Stesichorium   trimetrum acatalectum
56. Simonidium   trimetrum hypercatalectum
57. Alcmanium   tetrametrum brachycatalectum
58. Aristophanium   tetrametrum catalecticum

DE CHORIAMBICIS

59. Aristophanium   monometrum et antibacchum
60. Anacreontium   dimetrum et antibacchum
61. Sapphicum   trimetrum et antibacchum
62. Callimachium   tetrametrum et antibacchum

DE ANTISPASTICIS

63. Panicum   trimetrum brachycatalectum
64. Anacreontium   trimetrum catalecticum
65. Alcaicum   tetrametrum brachycatalectum
66. Anacreontium   tetrametrum catalecticum

DE IONICIS A MAIORE

67. Hipponactium   dimetrum brachycatalectum
68. Praxillum   trimetrum brachycatalectum
69. Sotadicum   tetrametrum brachycatalectum

DE IONICIS A MINORE

70. Timocratium   dimetrum catalecticum
71. Anacreontium   dimetrum acatalectum

72. Anacreontium		trimetrum catalecticum
73. Sapphicum		trimetrum acatalectum
74. Phrynichium		tetrametrum catalecticum
75. Alcmanium		tetrametrum acatalectum

DE DIVERSIS

76. Faliscum	(constat)	tribus dactylis et pyrrichio
77. Pherecratium	„	spondio dactylo spondio
78. Glyconium	„	spondio choriambo pyrrichio
79. Asclepiadium	„	spondio duobus choriambis pyrrichio
80. Alcaicum	„	spondio tribus choriambis pyrrichio
81. Elegiacum	„	penthemimeri prima heroica, secunda dactylica
82. Aeolicum	„	primo pede disyllabo quolibet et quattuor dactylis
83. Miurum	„	ut heroicum sed pyrrichio clauditur
84. Priapeium	„	glyconio et pherecratio
85. Phalaecium	„	spondio dactylo tribus trochaeis
86. Sapphicum	„	trochaeo spondio dactylo duobus trochaeis
87. Saturnium	„	dimetro iambico catalectico et ithyphallico
88. Archilochium	„	paroemiaco et ithyphallico
89. Encomiologicum	„	dactylica et iambica penthemimeri
90. Iambelegum	„	penthemimeri iambica et dactylica
91. Alcaicum	„	penthemimeri iambica et duobus dactylis
92. Alcaicum	„	duobus dactylis et duobus trochaeis
93. Archilochium	„	tetrametro bucolico et tribus trochaeis
94. Galliambicum	„	dimetro iambico catalectico et anapaesto vel spondio cum duobus iambis
95. Archilochium	„	penthemimeri dactylica et dimetro iambico acatalecto

96. Archilochium   ,,   dimetro iambico acatalecto et penthemimeri dactylica

97. Echoicum   quotiens sonus ultimae syllabae
paenultimae congruit

98. Reciprocum heroum   quotiens a fine scansus sotadicum
facit

99. Reciprocum iambicum quotiens a fine scansus elegiacum
facit

100. Ropalicus   cum verba, prout secuntur, per
syllabas crescunt.

The mathematical organization of sections one through eight is clear at a mere glance. Section nine, *de diversis*, calls for explanation. The following schematic outline will facilitate understanding.

DE DIVERSIS

76. Faliscium: 3 dactyls + pyrrhic
77. Pherecratium: spondee + dactyl + spondee
78. Glyconium: spondee + choriamb + pyrrhic
79. Asclepiadium: spondee + 2 choriambs + pyrrhic
80. Alcaicum: spondee + 3 choriambs + pyrrhic
81. Elegiacum: $2\frac{1}{2}$ spondees + $2\frac{1}{2}$ dactyls
82. Aeolicum: 2 syllables + 4 dactyls
83. Miurum: 5 dactyls + pyrrhic
84. Priapeium: spondee + choriamb + pyrrhic
               spondee + dactyl + spondee
85. Phalaecium: spondee + dactyl + 3 trochees
86. Sapphicum: trochee + spondee + dactyl + 2 trochees
87. Saturnium: iambic dimeter catalectic + ithyphallic
88. Archilochium: anapestic dimeter catalectic + ithyphallic
89. Encomiologic: dactylic penthemimer + iambic penthemimer
90. Iambelegum: iambic penthemimer + dactylic penthemimer
91. Alcaicum: iambic penthemimer + 2 dactyls
92. Alcaicum: 2 dactyls + 2 trochees
93. Archilochium: 4 dactyls + 3 trochees
94. Galliambicum: iambic dimeter acatalectic + anapest + 2
               iambs

95. Archilochium: dactylic penthemimer + iambic dimeter aca-
     talectic
96. Archilochium: iambic dimeter acatalectic + dactylic penthe-
     mimer
97. Echoicum: metrical tour de force
98. Reciprocum H: metrical tour de force
99. Reciprocum 1: metrical tour de force
100. Ropalicus: metrical tour de force

First of all, let us notice that the four Archilochian metres in question are numbers 13, 18, 20 and 21 of this section or metres 88, 93, 95 and 96 of the hundred metres. As in the case of other poets, the metres of Archilochus are not given a special placement juxtaposed by themselves. Again, as in the case of the previous eight sections, a logical pattern of organization governs the arrangement of the metres of section 9 without regard to the poets who employed them. The first group of metres which forms a unit includes 76 (faliscium) through 84 (priapeium). The metres of this group are generally composed of three parts. All either begin with a spondee and/or end with a pyrrhic. Especially obvious is the technique of juxtaposing 78, 79 and 80 (glyconium, asclepiadium and alcaicum) which have the same components save that the choriambic element increases from one, to two, to three. Metres 85 and 86 form a second group whose common components are spondee + dactyl + multiple trochees. Metres 87 and 88 (saturnium and archilochium) have as their basis catalectic dimeter and the ithyphallic. 89-91 are a penthemimer group. The last component of metre 91, the 2 dactyls, introduces the group 92 and 93 both of which begin with multiple dactyls which are followed by multiple trochees. 92 (alcaicum) with 2 dactyls + 2 trochees naturally introduces 93 (archilochium) with 4 dactyls + 3 trochees. 94 through 96 form another group whose unity is assured by the common element, the iambic dimeter acatalectic. Metre 94 (galliambicum) stands first with the largest number of iambs. 95 (archilochium) follows and is in turn followed by another Archilochian metre (96) which is its opposite. 97 through 100 comprise the last group whose unifying element is the metrical tour de force or oddity. Take, for example, 97 (echoicum): *sonus ultimae syllabae paenultimae congruit*; or 100 (ropalicus) in which each word is longer than its predecessor by a syllable:

rem tibi confeci, doctissime, dulcisonoram

Of the citations of the second metrician, Lasserre comments:

... Héphestion a consacré tout un chapitre, le quinzième de son abrégé, aux asynartètes et lui a donné le même plan, en ce qui concerne Archiloque, que Servius; il a toutefois omis le quatrième type — archiloquien 4 — et ajouté un archiloquien 5 qu'il tire des pieces douteuses qui étaient placées à la fin du livre des *Épodes*.[5]

As was the case with Servius we shall find that Hephaestion also arranged his *Enchiridion*[6] in a highly mechanistic fashion which explains the order in which Archilochian metres are cited. Let us first take a look at the table of contents of the entire manual:

Chapter	Contents
1	Περὶ συλλαβῶν
2	Περὶ συνεκφωνήσεως
3	Περὶ ποδῶν
4	Περὶ μέτρων
5	Περὶ ἰαμβικοῦ
6	Περὶ τροχαϊκοῦ
7	Περὶ δακτυλικοῦ
8	Περὶ ἀναπαιστικοῦ
9	Περὶ χοριαμβικοῦ
10	Περὶ ἀντισπαστικοῦ
11	Περὶ τοῦ ἀπὸ μείζονος ἰωνικοῦ
12	Περὶ τοῦ ἀπ' ἐλάσσονος ἰωνικοῦ
13	Περὶ παιωνικοῦ
14	Περὶ τῶν κατ' ἀντιπάθειαν μίξεων
15	Περὶ ἀσυναρτήτων
16	Περὶ πολυσχηματίστων
17	Περὶ ποιήματος

[5] *Op. cit.* (above, n.IV.1), 20.
[6] M. Consbruch, *Hephaestionis enchiridion* (Lipsiae, 1906).

Chapters 5-12 are arranged exactly as chapters 1-8 of Servius where the order is iamb, trochee, dactyl, anapest, choriamb, antispast, ionic a maiore, ionic a minore; and for the same reasons (above, 88-89). Hephaestion before treating diverse metres (14-17) includes another metrical foot, the paeon (–◡◡◡). Chapters 1-4 likewise show a logical progression from syllables, to synizesis, to feet, to metres.

We now turn our attention to chapter 15 which contains the four Archilochian metres in question:

Chapter 15: ASYNARTETE VERSES[7]

(A) Περὶ τῶν ἐπισυνθέτων

1. anapestic hephthemimer + ithyphallic
2. dactylic tetrapody   + ithyphallic
3. dactylic penthemimer + iambic dimeter acatalectic
4. dactylic penthemimer + iambic penthemimer
5. iambic penthemimer   + dactylic penthemimer
6. dactylic penthemimer + iambic penthemimer + dactylic penthemimer
7. iambic penthemimer   + dactylic penthemimer + iambic penthemimer

(B) Περὶ τοῦ μονοειδοῦς τοῦ καλουμένου ἐλεγείου

8. dactylic penthemimer   + dactylic penthemimer

(C) Περὶ τῶν ἀντιπαθῶν

9. iambic dimeter acatalectic   + trochaic hephthemimer
10. iambic dimeter acatalectic   + 3 trochees
11. trochaic dimeter acatalectic + iambic hephthemimer
12. choriamb + 2 iambs + ithyphallic
13. choriamb + 2 iambs + trochaic hephthemimer

(D) Περὶ τῶν μονοειδῶν καὶ τῶν ὁμοιοειδῶν

[7] I follow the sectioning of R. Westphal, *Scriptores metrici graeci* 1 (Lipsiae, 1866).

14. antispastic dimeter catalectic + antispastic dimeter catalectic
15. iambic hephthemimer   + iambic hephthemimer
16. ithyphallic   + ithyphallic
17. choriambic hephthemimer   + choriambic hephthemimer

The methodical fourfold grouping of the metres of chapter 15 is clear from the chart. Within the group labelled Περὶ τῶν ἐπισυνθέτων are included three of the Archilochian metres in question. The first seven metres are each an ἐπισύνθετος, that is, a metre composed of κῶλα of different kinds. By κῶλον is meant a metrical unit containing fewer than three pairs (συζυγίαι) without catalexis (Heph. Proem. 1). When we reduce the metres of the first group to their numerical equivalents the organization becomes clear:

1. $3\frac{1}{2}$ anapests + 3 trochees
2. 4   dactyls + 3 trochees
3. $2\frac{1}{2}$ dactyls + 4 iambs
4. $2\frac{1}{2}$ dactyls + $2\frac{1}{2}$ iambs
5. $2\frac{1}{2}$ iambs   + $2\frac{1}{2}$ dactyls
6. $2\frac{1}{2}$ dactyls + $2\frac{1}{2}$ iambs   + $2\frac{1}{2}$ dactyls
7. $2\frac{1}{2}$ iambs   + $2\frac{1}{2}$ dactyls + $2\frac{1}{2}$ iambs

Metres 1-5 are composed of two κῶλα each; metres 6 and 7 are composed of three κῶλα each and are the reverse of each other. Of 7 Hephaestion says: Ἀντεστραμμένον δε εστι τούτῳ (= metre 6) τὸ Πινδαρικὸν καλούμενον. Likewise, Hephaestion tells us that metre 5 is the reverse of metre 4. The arrangement of metres 1-4 is also clear. Hephaestion begins with 1 composed of two κῶλα, the first of which is $3\frac{1}{2}$ anapests and the second of which is 3 trochees. Metre 2 also has a second κῶλον of 3 trochees and introduces a first κῶλον of dactyls. Metre 3 then continues with a first dactylic κῶλον but has a second κῶλον of 4 iambs. Metre 4 also has a first dactylic κῶλον of $2\frac{1}{2}$ dactyls and a second iambic κῶλον, but the iambs have been reduced from 4 iambs in metre 3 to $2\frac{1}{2}$ iambs. We have already mentioned that metre 5 is the reverse of metre 4. The Archilochian metres 1-3 are therefore simply placed in their appropriate schematic positions and yield no inference with regard to their order in the Archilochian text.

The fourth Archilochian metre (Lasserre calls it archiloquien 5) included in chapter 15 is metre 9, the first metre of section C Περί τῶν ἀντιπαθῶν. Consider the arrangement of this section. As the title suggests and the scholia explain,[8] the contrast is between the iambic components and the trochaic components. Hence, asynartete verses in which this occurs are catalogued in this section. Metres 9-11 have two components; metres 12-13 have three components:

9. 4 iambs $+ 3\frac{1}{2}$ trochees
10. 4 iambs $+ 3$ trochees
11. 4 trochees $+ 3\frac{1}{2}$ iambs
12. choriamb $+ 2$ iambs $+ 3$ trochees
13. choriamb $+ 2$ iambs $+ 3\frac{1}{2}$ trochees

Hephaestion begins with the Archilochian metre (9) composed of 4 iambs and $3\frac{1}{2}$ trochees, and notes that the metre of 10 is the same minus one syllable. 11 reverses the iambic and trochaic components. 12 and 13 are composed of three components and are the same save that one syllable has been added to the end of 13, as Hephaestion notes.

Lasserre's third metrician is Marius Plotius Sacerdos, author of *artes grammaticae* in three books, the third of which is entitled *de metris*.[9] Lasserre simply says:

Marius Plotius, renversant l'ordre, décrit dans son chapitre 11 aux paragraphes 4, 7, et 10 (Gaisford) successivement les archiloquiens 3, 2, 1.[10]

Let us employ the same techniques of structural examination as were used in the cases of Servius and Hephaestion.

The organization of the *de metris* by chapters is again the mechanistic and logical organization we have seen in both Servius and Hephaestion:

[8] Scholia A, Περὶ ἀσυναρτήτων (52.24) on κατὰ τὴν πρώτην ἀντιπάθειαν comments: οἷον εἰ ἀντὶ ‹τοῦ› ἀπὸ βραχείας ἀρχῆς ἰάμβου ὁ ἀπὸ μακρᾶς τροχαῖος παραληφθείη.
[9] H. Keil, *Grammatici latini* 6 (Lipsiae, 1874).
[10] *Op. cit.* (above, VI,n.1), 20.

Chapter   Contents

1   de pedibus
2   de metris
3   de dactylico metro
4   de iambico metro
5   de metro trochaico
6   de metro anapaestico
7   de choriambico metro
8   de antispastico metro
9   de ionico metro
10   de paeonico metro
11   de metris compositis
12   de asynartetis metris

Chapter 3, *de dactylico metro*, is the only item out of the expected order. Normally, it should be placed between chapters 5 and 6, the trochaic and anapestic metres. The reason for placing the dactylic metre first is apparent from the metrician's comment: Dactylicum metrum omnibus et simplicius et antiquius est (3.3.1). When he resumes the normal order with chapter 4, the metrician explains: Iambicum non ut dactylicum simplex est, sed varium (3.4.1).

The following table lists the metres of chapter 11 with their components:

1. Iambelegum: iambic penthemimer + dactylic penthemimer
2. Encomiologicum
   stesichorium: dactylic penthemimer + iambic penthemimer
3. Encomiologicum
   archilochium: dactylic penthemimer + 4 iambs
4. Logaoedicum
   archebulium: 2 dactyls + 2 trochees (or trochee + spondee)
5. Hemiepes
   archebulium: 2 dactyls + 1 spondee
6. Logaoedicum
   archilochium: 4 dactyls + 3 trochees
7. Compositum

pindaricum: iambic penthemimer + dactylic penthemimer + iambic penthemimer

8. Compositum
susarionium: 4 trochees + dactylic penthemimer
9. Prosodiacum
hyporchematicum: syllable + dactylic penthemimer + syllable + 3 trochees

Metres 1-3: Marius Plotius Sacerdos begins the chapter, *de metris compositis*, with the iambelegum and notes that the reverse of this metre is the encomiologicum of Stesichorus. The encomiologicum of Archilochus with its dactylic penthemimer + 4 iambs naturally follows the encomiologicum of Stesichorus with its dactylic penthemimer + iambic penthemimer. Metres 4-6: the logaoedic group. The basic components are multiple dactyls + the trochee and/or spondee. The progression is mathematical from 2 dactyls to 4 dactyls, and from 2 trochees in metre 4 to 3 trochees in metre 6. The spondee in 5 naturally follows upon the possible spondee in 4. Metres 7-8: the compositum group. The common element is the dactylic penthemimer. Metre 9: the prosodiacum. This metre shares with metre 8 the dactylic penthemimer, and multiple trochees in reverse position. Note that the metre is simply called the prosodiacum hyporchematicum on which Marius Victorinus says: quia aptum saltantibus videtur, hyporchematicon a Graecis dicitur.[11] Neither metrician mentions Archilochus in connection with this metre.

The position of the three Archilochian metres was then determined purely by the schematic arrangement of the chapter. Metre 3, the encomiologicum archilochium, is placed with the encomiologicum group. Metre 6, the logaoedicum archilochium, is placed with the logaoedic group. Metre 9 is not labeled as Archilochian and there is therefore no evidence that Sacerdos was thinking of Archilochus in connection with this metre.

Lasserre's *Les Épodes d'Archiloque* provided the basis for the Epodes as they appear in *Archiloque. Fragments*[12] in which the text

[11]   *Ars grammatica* 2.8.
[12]   Paris, 1958.

is that of Lasserre himself, with translation and commentary by Andre Bonnard. Reviewers have questioned various reconstructions of the epodes[13] and we will here deal only with one epode (which Lasserre calls epode 11) which indicates how the "metrical evidence" has had its chain reaction. Once Lasserre had assumed that the citations of the metricians followed the metrical order of the epodes, he then felt safe in assuming that Horace in epodes 11-16 was closely imitating Archilochian metrical order and contents. Hence it is possible for Lasserre to restore the Archilochian epode by picking and choosing among those fragments which were metrically convenient and had a somewhat similar content. The process is skeptically summed up by Bonnard in his commentary on LB fragments 260-265:

> Si l'on est tenté d'attribuer à une même épode nos fragments 260 à 265, c'est en se fondant sur l'hypothèse qu'Horace aurait emprunté à cette onzième épode d'Archiloque (si elle a existé) son thème, sa composition et sa forme métrique.[14]

The text and translation of LB fragment 260 are:

$- \cup\cup - \cup\cup - \cup\cup -$ ἔξωθεν ἕκαστος
ἔπινεν. ἐν δὲ βακχίη $- \cup\cup - \cup\cup \overline{\cup}$
‹A l'abri de la tempête› du dehors, chacun buvait et, dedans, c'était Bacchus déchaîné.

Fragment 260 comes from a grammarian in Welcker's *Opuscula* where no reference is made to its metre. Bergk (83 and Diehl 111) considered it a tetrameter and emended it to read:

[13] J. Pouilloux, *REA* 60 (1958), 421-424, in a very general review which does not come to grips with the issues raised in LB labels their work "... aussi précise que prudente, et désormais indispensable". F. Jouan, *RBPh* 38 (1960), 577-579, lauds the introduction. For more representative reviews see K. J. Dover, *CR* 10 (1960), 10-12, especially on LB epode 1, and J. A. Davison, *JHS* 80 (1960), 202-203, who "unsparingly condemns" the practice of (a) separation of quotations from their contexts, and (b) the arrangements of fragments to suit a particular theory of their interpretation. G. W. Bond, *Gnomon* 32 (1960), 596-600, concludes: "The fundamental defect of the editors is simply an inadequate sense of what is probable and what is not. Their book is an admixture of what is certain, probable, improbable, and (on occasion) impossible: the reader must work hard to find and to test the links in the chain of evidence." See also G. Morelli, "Una nuova edizione di Archiloco", *Maia* 12 (1960), 130-153.

[14] Adrados, *op. cit.* (above, VI, n. 4), 70-75, denies the existence of Lasserre's epodes 11 and 14. See also Adrados' review, *Paideia* 14 (1959), 267-272.

ἔξωθεν ἔκαστος ἔπινεν   ἐν δὲ βακχίη‹σιν›
˘‒ ˘ ˘ ‒ ˘ ˘ ‒ ˘   ‒ ˘ ‒ ˘‒ ˘

which is a paroemiac and ithyphallic line. Lasserre insists (properly, it seems to me) on leaving the fragment unemended. The
difficulty, however, is how to place the fragment. Lasserre presumes
that the fragment is related to the beginning of Horace's thirteenth
epode. Hence for him ἔξωθεν ἔκαστος constitutes the end of a
hexameter and ἔπινεν the beginning of an iambic dimeter. The
next step is to separate ἔξωθεν from ἔκαστος ἔπινεν and connect
the adverb with the storm in *horrida tempestas* of Horace 13.1. The
idea of a storm in Archilochus is gratuitously supplied from the
storm in Horace. The translation (à l'abri de la tempête) of
Bonnard is curious for there is no such parallel phrase in Horace
13.[15] The restoration is completely gratuitous. But let us return
to the question of metre. Rivier argues convincingly:

> Cette lecture du fragment n'est pas recevable: elle introduit une "ponc-
> tuation", au sens que les métriciens donnent à ce terme, après le 5ᵉ
> trochée, ce qui est contraire aux lois de l'hexamètre (cf. P. Maas, *Griech.
> Metrik* #88). ... ici c'est la considération du mètre qui récuse la thèse du
> parallelisme stricte entre Archiloque et Horace.[16]

But there is another problem still to be considered, for granting that
ἔξωθεν ἔκαστος constitutes the end of a hexameter (though not
granting the punctuation after ἔξωθεν) ἔπινεν ἐν δὲ βακχίη may
˘‒ ˘ ‒ ˘ ‒ ˘
be a simple line of pure iambic dimeter and in that case the distich
is in fact simply a first pythiambic, a couplet of dactylic hexameter
and iambic dimeter which is the metre of Horace's fourteenth and
fifteenth epodes and not that of the thirteenth. None of the other
supposed fragments of LB's Archilochus 11 are anything but
dactylic hexameter and hence Lasserre has failed to even demonstrate that his fragments yield the metre of Horace 13.[17]

[15]   On Bonnard's translations see B. A. Van Groningen, *Mnemosyne* 12
(1959), 148-149, who speaks of a "traduction élégante, encore que parfois
très libre", and J. Meunier, *AC* 30 (1961), 191-194, who offers some reser-
vations à propos of the translations.
[16]   *Op. cit.* (above, VI, n. 3), 467.
[17]   For further arguments against the content relationship of LB fragments
260-265 to Horace 13 see Stoessel, *AJP* 74 (1953), 300-301. For possible non-
Archilochian sources of Horace 13 see Kirn, *op. cit.* (above, n.IV.10), 57-59,
and Fraenkel, *op. cit.* (above, n.IV.11), 65-66.

To conclude, the influence of the Archilochian *Epodes* upon the Horatian *Epodes* both with regard to metrical order and thematic sequence remains for lack of evidence a mystery, save for instances where the standard studies or commentaries have prudently suggested or established a relationship, close or loose as the case may be.[18]

---

[18]   Fraenkel, *op. cit.*, (above, n.IV.11), 24-36, on epode 10 is an excellent illustration. Interestingly enough, the relationship is extremely loose and the metres are different . LB consider this Greek fragment (Diehl 79a) to belong to Hipponax and omit it. For solid additional support of Archilochian authorship of the fragment see G. M. Kirkwood, "The Authorship of the Strasbourg Epodes", *TAPA* 92 (1961), 267-282.

BIBLIOGRAPHY

Adrados, F., "Nueva reconstrucción de los epodos de Arquíloco", *Emerita* 23 (1955), 1-78.
——, Review of Lasserre-Bonnard's *Archiloque. Fragments, Paideia* 14 (1959), 267-272.
Allen, S., "On Horace, Epode XV., 1-10; and on Virgil, *Aeneid* IX., 339", *CR* 16 (1902), 305-306.
Alton, E. H., "The Zeugma in Horace *Epode* XV", *CR* 19 (1905), 215-216.
Axelson, B., "Eine Crux Interpretum in den Epoden des Horaz (XVI, 15-16)", *Ut pictura poesis. Studia latina P. J. Enk septuagenario oblata* (Leiden 1955), 45-52.
Barwick, K., "Zur Interpretation und Chronologie der 4. Ecloge des Vergil usw.", *Philologus* 96 (1943), 28-67.
Becker, C., "Vergils Eklogenbuch", *Hermes* 83 (1955), 314-349.
Belling, H., *Untersuchung der Elegien des Albius Tibullus* (Berlin, 1897).
——, *Studien über die Liederbücher des Horatius* (Berlin, 1903).
Bennett, C. E. -Rolfe, J. C., *Horace. Complete Works* (Boston, 1901).
Bentley, R., *Q. Horatius Flaccus* (Cantabrigiae, 1711).
Boissier, G., *Nouvelles promenades archéologiques* (Paris, 1886).
Boll, F., "Die Anordnung im zweiten Buch von Horaz' *Satiren*", *Hermes* 48 (1913), 143-145.
Bond, G. W., Review of Lasserre-Bonnard's *Archiloque. Fragments, Gnomon* 32 (1960), 596-600.
Botschuyver, H. J., *Scholia in Horatium* λφψ *codicum parisinorum latinorum* 7972, 7974, 7971 (Amstelodami, 1935).
——, *Scholia in Horatium* χI *in codicibus parisinis 'latinis 17897 et 8223 obvia* (Amstelodami, 1942).
Brunori, G., *La lingua d'Orazio* (Firenze, 1930).
Buchheit, V., "Horazens programmatische Epode (VI)", *Gymnasium* 68 (1961), 520-526.
Buecheler, F., "Coniectanea", *Index scholarum hib.* (Bonnae, 1878/9), 3-26.
Büchner, K., "Dichtung und Grammatik", *Mnemosyne* 10 (1957), 22-34.
Cahen, R., Review of Pluss' *Das Jambenbuch des Horaz, Bulletin Critique* 5 (1905), 91-97.
Cahn, S., *Trias quaestionum horatianarum* (Bonnae, 1838).
Campbell, A. Y., *Horace. A New Interpretation* (London, 1924).
——, *Horace. Odes and Epodes*² (Liverpool, 1953).

——, "The Structure of Horace's Ninth Epode", *PCA* 51 (1954), 55.

Carcopino, J., *Daily Life in Ancient Rome* (tr. E. O. Lorimer, London, 1941).

Carrubba, R., "A Study of Horace's Eighth and Twelfth Epodes", *Latomus* 24 (1965), 591-598.

——, "The Metrical Order of the Archilochian Epodes", *Emerita* 33 (1965), 61-70.

——, "Horace's Fifteenth Epode: An Interpretation", *Acta Antiqua* 13 (1965), 417-423.

——, "Horace, *Epod*. 2.49-60", *CB* 41 (1965), 62-63.

——, "La Structure de la troisième Épode d'Horace", *LEC* 33 (1965), 412-417.

Christ, W., *Horatiana* (Munich, 1893).

Cobet, C. G., "Ad leg. 1. D. *ad legem Iuliam de vi privata*. Lex Roscia. Lex Iulia theatralis", *Mnemosyne* 10 (1861), 337-342.

Collinge, N. E., "Form and Content in the Horatian Lyric", *CP* 50 (1955), 161-168.

——, *The Structure of Horace's Odes* (London, 1961).

Colmant, P., "Horace, *Épode* III", *LEC* 25 (1957), 107-109.

Commager, S., *The Odes of Horace. A Critical Study* (New Haven, 1962).

Consbruch, M., *Hephaestionis enchiridion* (Lipsiae, 1906).

Cooper, L., *A Concordance to the Works of Horace* (Washington, 1916).

Costa, E., *Il diritto nei poeti di Roma* (Bologna, 1898).

Cruquius, J., *Q. Horatius Flaccus cum commentariis et enarrationibus commentatoris veteris, et Iacobi Cruquii Messenii* (Leiden, 1597).

Crusius, O., "Zu den Canidia-Epoden des Horaz", *Philologus* 53 (1894), 79.

Curcio, G., "La tesi dell'Epodo 2 di Q. Orazio Flacco". *Miscellanea di studi critici in onore di Ettore Stampini* (Torino, 1921), 29-34.

D'Alton, J. F., *Horace and His Age. A Study in Historical Background* (London, 1917).

Di Bella, A., "Il passo dell'Epodo V. di Orazio (vv. 87-88)", *Studi critici offerti da antichi discepoli a Carlo Pascal nel suo* XXV *anno d'insegnamento* (Catania, 1935).

Dover, K. J., Review of Lasserre-Bonnard's *Archiloque. Fragments*, *CR* 10 (1960), 10-12.

Drew, D. L., "Horace, *Epodes* V. 49-82", *CR* 37 (1923), 24-25.

Drexler, H., "Interpretationen zu Horaz' 16. Epode.", *SIFC* 12 (1935), 119-164.

Duckworth, G. E., "*Animae Dimidium Meae*: Two Poets of Rome", *TAPA* 87 (1956), 281-316.

——, "Recent Work on Vergil (1940-1956), IV-V", *CW* 51 (1958), 123-128.

Düntzer, H., "Des Horatius Canidia-Gedichte", *JKP* 145 (1892), 597-613.

Eitrem, S., "La magie comme motif littéraire chez les Grecs et les Romains", *SO* 21 (1941), 39-83.

Fahz, L., *De poetarum romanorum doctrina magica* (Numburgi, 1904).

Ferrabino, A., "La battaglia d'Azio", *RFIC* 2 (1924), 433-472.

Fraenkel, E., "Carattere della poesia augustea", *Maia* 1 (1948), 245-264.

——, *Horace* (Oxford, 1957).

Frank, T., "Vergil's Apprenticeship", *CP* 15 (1920), 23-38.

——, *Vergil. A Biography* (New York, 1922).

Franke, C., *Fasti horatiani* (Berlin, 1839).

Funaioli, G., "Horatiana", *Mélanges de philologie, de littérature et d'histoire anciennes offerts à J. Marouzeau par ses collègues et élèves étrangers* (Paris, 1948), 183-188.

Giarratano, C., *Il libro degli Epodi* (Torino, 1930).

Graf, M., "Die 15. Epode des Horaz", *Xenien* (München, 1891), 13-19.

Grimm, J., *The Construction ΑΠΟ ΚΟΙΝΟΥ in the Works of Horace* (Philadelphia, 1928).

Grotefend, G., *Die schriftstellerische Laufbahn des Horatius* (Hannover, 1849).

Hahn, E. A., "*Epodes* 5 and 17. *Carmina* 1.16 and 1.17", *TAPA* 70 (1939), 213-230.

——, "The Characters in the *Eclogues*", *TAPA* 75 (1944), 196-241.

Haight, E. H., "A Note In Horace's Second Epode", *CW* 4 (1918), 44-45.

Hancock, E., "The Use of the Singular *Nos* by Horace", *CQ* 19 (1925), 43-55.

Hardie, W. R., "On Horace, *Epodes V.* 29-31", *CR* 20 (1906), 115.

Harnecker, O., "Der 14. Epodos des Horatius", *ZG* 36 (1882), 428-433.

Hauthal, F., *Acronis et Porphyrionis commentarii in Q. Horatium Flaccum*, 2 vols. (Berolini, 1864).

Henriot, E., *Mœurs juridiques et judiciaires de l'ancienne Rome d'après les poetes latins*, 3 vols. (Paris, 1865).

Herrmann, L., *Horace. Épodes* (Berchem-Bruxelles, 1953).

Housman, A. E., "Horatiana", *JP* 10 (1882), 187-196.

——, "Elucidations of Latin Poets", *CR* 15 (1901), 404-406.

——, "Horace. *Épode* XIII 3.", *CR* 37 (1923), 104.

Hubaux, J., "La sérénade de l'amant vengé", *AC* 4 (1935), 349-356.

Juan, F., Review of Lasserre-Bonnard's *Archiloque. Fragments*, *RBPh* 38 (1960), 577-579.

Keil, H., *Grammatici latini* 6 (Lipsiae, 1874).

Keller, O., *Pseudoacronis scholia on Horatium vetustiora* 1 (Lipsiae, 1902).

Keller, O.-Holder, A., *Q. Horati Flacci Opera. Carminum libri* IIII. *Epodon liber. Carmen saeculare* (Lipsiae, 1899).

Kent, R. G., "Notes on Latin Authors", *Studies Presented to David Moore Robinson* (Saint Louis, 1953), 686-692.

Kiessling, A.-Heinze, R., *Q, Horatius Flaccus. Satiren*[7] (Berlin, 1959).

——, *Q. Horatius Flaccus. Oden und Epoden*[10] (Berlin, 1960).

Kirchner, C., *Quaestiones horatianae* (Numburgi, 1834).

Kirkwood, G., "The Authorship of the Strasbourg Epodes", *TAPA* 92 (1961), 267-282.

Kirn, B., *Zur literarischen Stellung von Horazens Jambenbuch* (Tübingen, 1935).

Koldewey, F., "Figura ἀπὸ κοινοῦ bei Catull, Tibull, Properz und Horaz", *ZG* 31 (1877), 337-358.

Kroll, J., "Horaz Epode XVI und Vergils Bukolika", *Hermes* 57 (1922), 600-612.

Kroll, W., *Studien zum Verständnis der römischen Literatur* (Stuttgart, 1924).

Kromayer, J., "Forschungen zur Geschichte des II. Triumvirats", *Hermes* 34 (1899), 1-54.

——, "Actium. Ein Epilog", *Hermes* 68 (1933), 361-383.

Kukula, R. C., *Römische Säkularpoesie. Neue Studien zu Horaz' 16. Epodus und Vergils 4. Ekloge* (Leipzig, 1911).

Kumaniecki, C. F., "De epodis quibusdam horatianis", *Commentationes horatianae* (Cracoviae, 1935).

Kurfess, A., "Zu Horazens 16. Epode", *PhW* 45 (1925), 604-606.

——, "Bemerkungen zu Horazens Jambenbuch", *PhW* 55 (1935), 844-848.

——, "Vergil und Horaz", *ZRGG* 6 (1954), 359-364.

Lasserre, F., *Les Épodes d'Archiloque* (Paris, 1950).

Lasserre, F.-Bonnard, A., *Archiloque. Fragments* (Paris, 1958).

Latsch, R., *Die Chronologie der Satiren und Epoden des Horaz auf entwicklungsgeschichtlicher Grundlage* (Würzburg, 1936).

Lee, A. G., Review of Wistrand's *Horace's Ninth Epode*, *Gnomon* 31 (1959), 740-741.

Ludwig, W., "Zu Horaz, C. 2.1-12", *Hermes* 85 (1957), 336-345.

——, "Die Anordnung des vierten Horazischen Odenbuches", *MH* 18 (1961), 1-10.

Marx, F., "Critica et hermeneutica", *RhM* 83 (1934), 372-384.

Maury, P., "Le secret de Virgile et l'architecture des Bucoliques", *Lettres d'Humanité* 3 (1944), 71-147.

Miniconi, P., "Les proportions mathématiques dans l'Éneide", *Latomus* 22 (1963), 263-273.

Moseley, J., "Did Horace Study Law?" *TAPA* 66 (1935), xxix.

Mueller, L., *Q. Horatius Flaccus. Oden und Epoden* (Leipzig, 1900).

Murison, A. F., "The Law in the Latin Poets", *Atti del congresso internazionale di Diritto Romano* 2 (Pavia, 1935), 609-639.

Naylor, H. D., "Latin Poetic Order, with Special Reference to Horace *Epodes* 5. 19.", *CR* 32 (1918), 161-162.

——, *Horace. Odes and Epodes. A Study in Poetic Word-Order* (Cambridge, 1922).

Nettleship, H., *Lectures and Essays* (Oxford, 1885).

Noirfalise, A., "Horace, chevalier romain", *LEC* 18 (1950), 16-21.

Nonn, "Die Komposition der zweiten Epode des Horaz". *PhW* 40 (1920), 1124-1127.

O'Brien, J., "Horace, Champion of the Country", *CB* 37 (1961), 33-35.

Olivier, F., *Les Épodes d'Horace* (Lausanne, 1917).

Orelli, J. G.-Baiter, J. G.-Hirschfelder, G., *Q. Horatius Flaccus* 1 (Berlin, 1886).

Orth, E., "Obeloi", *PhW* 55 (1935), 111.

Page, T. E., *Q. Horatii Flacci. Carminum libri IV. Epodon liber* (London, 1959).

Paladini, M., "A proposito della tradizione poetica sulla battaglia di Azio", *Latomus* 17 (1958), 240-269, 462-475.

Pasquali, G., *Orazio lirico* (Firenze, 1920).

Perret, J., *Horace* (Paris, 1959).

Plessis, F., *Q. Horati Flacci Carmina. Odes, Épodes, et Chant séculaire* (Paris, 1924).

Plüss, T., *Das Jambenbuch des Horaz* (Leipzig, 1904).

——, "Horazens *Beatus ille*", *ZG* 1 (1913), 83-92.

Pohl. J. C., "Der 14. Epodos des Horatius", *ZG* 33 (1879), 575-586.

Port, W., "Die Anordnung in Gedichtbüchern augusteischer Zeit", *Philologus* 81 (1925), 280-308.

Postgate, J. P., "On Horace Epode XV. 5 and Seneca *Herc. Oet.* 335 sqq.", *CR* 19 (1905), 217-218.

Raubitschek, A., "Phryne", *RE* 20 (1941), 893-907.

Rémy, L., "Horace, *Épode* II", *LEC* 26 (1958), 266-272.

Richardson, G. W., "Actium", *JRS* 27 (1937), 153-164.

108   BIBLIOGRAPHY

Rivier, A., Review of Lasserre's *Les Épodes d'Archiloque*, *REG* 65 (1952), 464-468.
Rolfe, J. C., "*A* or *AB* in Horace, Epod. 17.24.", *CR* 14 (1900), 261.
Rotondi, G., *Leges publicae populi romani* (Milano, 1912).
Salanitro, N., *L'epodo secondo di Orazio* (Catania, 1935).
Schmidt, M., "Das Epodenbuch des Horaz", *PhW* 52 (1932), 1005-1010.
Schweikert, E., "Der lyrische Aufbau der ersten Epode des Horatius", *JKP* 39 (1893), 638-640.
Sellar, W. Y., *The Roman Poets of the Augustan Age. Horace and the Elegiac Poets*² (Oxford, 1899).
Shorey, P.-Laing, G. L., *Horace. Odes and Epodes* (Chicago, 1919).
Siess, A., *Zu den Epoden des Horaz* (Graz, 1875).
Silk, E. T., "Cicero and the Odes of Horace", *YClS* 13 (1952), 145-158.
Skutsch, O., "The Structure of the Propertian Monobiblos", *CP* 58 (1963), 238-239.
Stella Maranca, F., "Per lo studio del diritto romano nell'opera di Orazio", *Archivio giuridico "Filippo Serafini"* 13 (1935), 31-88.
——, "Introduzione allo studio del Diritto Romano nell'opera di Orazio", *Historia* 9 (1935), 3-21, 369-400, 531-573.
——, "Orazio e la legislazione romana", *Conferenze Oraziane* (Milan, 1936), 43-66.
Stoessel, F., Review of Lasserre's *Les Épodes d'Archiloque AJP* (1953), 296-302.
Syme, R., *The Roman Revolution* (Oxford, 1960).
Tarn, W. W., "The Battle of Actium", *JRS* 21 (1931), 173-199.
——, "Antony's Legions", *CQ* 26 (1932), 75-81.
——, "Actium: A Note", *JRS* 28 (1938), 165-168.
Taylor, L. R., "Horace's Equestrian Career", *AJP* 46 (1925), 161-169.
Tescari, O., *Quinto Orazio Flacco. I Carmi e gli Epodi* (Torino, 1936).
Teuffel, W., "Ueber die Abfassungszeit der Horazischen Epoden", *ZA* 64-66 (1844) 508-525; 75-77 (1845), 596-616.
Tracy, H. L., "Thought-Sequence in the Ode", *Phoenix* 5 (1951) 108-118 [= *Studies in Honor of Gilbert Norwood* (Toronto, 1952) 203-213].
Turolla, E., *Q. Orazio Flacco. I Giambi* (Torino, 1957).
Ussani, V., *Le liriche di Orazio*² 1 (Torino, 1922).
Villeneuve, F., *Horace. Odes et Épodes* (Paris, 1927).
Wagenvoort, H., "De Horatii epodo nono", *Mnemosyne* 59 (1932), 403-421.
——, *Studies in Roman Literature, Religion and Culture* (Leiden, 1956).
Weinreich, O., *Römische Satiren* (Zürich, 1949).
Westphal, R., *Scriptores metrici graeci* 1 (Lipsiae, 1866).
Wickham, E. C., *The Works of Horace*³ 1 (Oxford, 1896).
Wickham, E. C.-Garrod, H. W., *Q. Horati Flacci Opera* (Oxonii, 1959).
Wili, W., *Horaz und die augusteische Kultur* (Basel, 1948).
Wilkinson, L. P., "Horace, Epode IX", *CR* 47 (1933) 2-6.
——, *Horace and His Lyric Poetry* (Cambridge, 1951).
Wistrand, E., *Horace's Ninth Epode and its Historical Background* (Göteborg, 1958).
Witte, K., "Horazens sechzente Epode und Vergils Bucolica", *PhW* 41 (1921), 1095-1103.

——, *Die Geschichte der römischen Dichtung in Zeitalter des Augustus*, II: *Horaz* (Erlangen, 1931).

Wurzel, F., "Der Ausgang der Schlacht von Aktium und die 9. Epode des Horaz", *Hermes* 73 (1938), 361-379.

Zielinski, T., "L'envoûtement de la sorcière chez Horace", *Mélanges offerts à O. Navarre par ses élèves et ses amis* (Toulouse, 1935).

——, *Horace et la société romaine du temps d'Auguste* (Paris, 1938).

INDEX